THE KING'S WISDOM

THE KING'S WISDOM

A HANDBOOK & DEVOTIONAL FOR 21st CENTURY CHRISTIANS

Paul Ige Adeyanju & Greg Mann

A heartfelt thank you to NormaJean Lutz of Notations Un-limited Writing Services for her invaluable editorial assistance and meticulous attention to detail, ensuring our book is polished and beautifully presented. And special thanks to Mardy Ross for her essential support and thoughtful editorial insights throughout this process. We couldn't have done it without you both!

Scripture references were drawn from the KJV, NKJV, NIV, NLT, and The Living Bible.

FIRST EDITION 2024

ISBN: 9798344167749
Imprint: 7 AM Books
Text Design by Paul Ige Adeyanju
Book cover by Greg Mann

10 11 12 13 OV/RRD 10 9 8 7 6 5 4 3 2 1

Contents

Introduction

WHEN I WAS JUST FIVE YEARS OLD, my mother received a prophetic word that her last child would speak before many people in foreign lands. The person who gave her the prophecy had no idea that her youngest child was actually a set of twins. To this day, she reminds me of that prophecy. At the time, it seemed impossible. Fast forward to 2009, and I'm standing in an airport in Nigeria, a kid fresh out of high school with the weight of that prophecy strapped to my back like a heavy backpack. My father gave me a hug and a pat on the shoulder that felt heavier than it should have, and before I knew it, I was boarding a plane to the United States of America alone. Fifteen hours and a few turbulence-filled prayers later, I landed in a world that was as foreign to me as snow in Lagos.

It would be six long years before my twin brother joined me here in the States, and fifteen even longer years before I'd see my parents again. I wish I could tell you that those years flew by like a montage in a movie, but they didn't. They dragged. There were moments when the weight of homesickness was so thick, it felt like I was drowning in a pool where no one knew I was sinking. In that time, I had no choice but to grow. Life in America wasn't the dreamland it's often painted to be. It was a grind—a relentless, unforgiving machine of school deadlines, rent payments, missed calls to family, and the awkward, biting loneliness of a culture that wasn't mine.

But through it all, one thing remained constant: God's presence. I had to trust that the same God who had plucked me from the warm, chaotic bustle of Nigeria had a plan. It was the only way to keep my sanity intact. I threw myself into school, work, and a different life entirely. Alone, but never truly alone. God, in His strange, often puzzling way, sent people in my direction. Strangers who became family. Friends who turned into lifelines. They were His way of reminding me that even in the darkest moments, there's always a flicker of light if we're willing to look for it.

It was during those early days that God began to stir something in me. His voice, soft but persistent, nudged me to write. Not novels - not yet - but short messages, sermons, things that felt like whispers from Heaven itself. He was teaching me something about preparation. David, the shepherd boy, came to mind often. Anointed to be king, he spent years battling lions and bears in the wilderness before his moment arrived. (And no, I didn't have any lions to fight in Florida—though my financial hardships hunted me like predators).

David's preparation wasn't just an accident. Every day with that sling and stone was leading up to the moment he'd stand before Goliath. In the same way, I felt like God was molding me, encouraging me that my time would come, and that I should be ready when it did. As the years rolled on, opportunities began to surface. I found myself standing before congregations, sharing the Word, and each time, the memory of the prophecy given to my mother would resurface. Like a quiet tap on my shoulder, it reminded me what had been said all those years ago. It wasn't flashy. There were no spotlights, no grand stages—just me, the pulpit, and a message burning in my heart.

Today, as I write these words, I serve as one of the worship leaders at my church. Sometimes I get the opportunity to share the Word of God. Sometimes I just stand there, overwhelmed by the strange, winding journey that's brought me here. I've spoken before people in this foreign land, just like the prophecy foretold, and spent five years serving as a chaplain and youth pastor at a school for at-risk teenagers. And beyond anything I could ever have imagined, I've been able to help my family in ways that once seemed impossible.

Here's the thing: God's timing? It's never early, never late. It's maddening, sure, but it's always perfect. His plan for me—His plan for you—is more intricate than we can ever understand. It may not always make sense while we're in the thick of it, but trust me, when you're able to look back, you'll see it. Every trial, every tear, every quiet victory— they all serve a purpose. Your life isn't a random sequence of events. It's a story being written by the Author of all things. But here's the catch—you have to stay obedient. Stay faithful. Stay prepared. David didn't just sit around waiting for Goliath to come to him. He trained. He worked. He fought. And when his moment came, he was ready.

This devotional you hold, *The King's Wisdom*, isn't just ink on paper. It's a collection of words that are ready to speak into your life, just as God has spoken into mine. The Bible tells us, "A word fitly spoken is like apples of gold in settings of silver." (Proverbs 25:11) I believe these words, these reflections, will be that timely word for you. They'll lift you when you're low, challenge you when you're comfortable, and prepare you for the battles ahead.

- **Paul Ige Adeyanju**

I WAS BORN IN BANGOR, MAINE IN 1959, but I've come to understand that I belonged to God long before that and will always belong to God. I accepted Jesus Christ as my Savior on a dark Colorado mountain road in 1981, when He stopped me in my tracks while I was hitchhiking and filled me with the knowledge of His love. From the beginning, experiences with the supernatural have been normal occurrences in my life. I was raised in a non-Christian family, the son of an award-winning aerospace engineer, and had my first encounter with something from beyond when I was seven years old.

After my father put me to bed one night, an apparition appeared on my wall—an enormous grinning face that stared down at me with a wicked leer until I mustered the courage to pull the covers over my head and turn over. After that experience, the sense that life plays out on a battlefield between two opposing forces has never left me. Two years later, my family moved into the mountains outside of Denver and life changed dramatically. The wild and scenic environment fueled my already creative imagination, and if I wasn't hiking, I was hunched over an old Royal typewriter banging out science fiction stories and drawing illustrations to go along with them.

A few years after graduating from high school, I picked up a girlfriend who dragged a guitar into the car behind her and said, "You should learn how to play this." I had never thought about playing the guitar, but this was God orchestrating things, and within a few years I grew confident enough to play and sing at small parties. Suddenly, for the first time, I had a clear vision for the future. I knew I was a one-man creative force. I could write, draw, sing and play an instrument - and all of these gifts were certainly bound to take me somewhere. God had a different plan, though. Or rather, some bad choices on my part forced God to adjust His plan. I lost everything overnight, guitar included, and ended up moving to a part of the country that was so foreign to me I felt as though I'd landed on the moon. It would be ten more years before I'd feel like I was on course again.

Credit for helping me turn my life around goes to a woman named Rosemary, who oversaw a prayer ministry aimed primarily at prodigals—which I most certainly was. That encounter, and the relationship that developed from it, remains one of the cruxes of my life. Everything is "before Rosemary," or "after Rosemary," in my mind, and I'm sure in God's mind also.

The first thing Rosemary taught me was how to pray, and especially how to make intercession. She was so diligent, committed, and fiery! When she prayed, things would change. Not only that, but she would share with me daily things that God had spoken to her. I was stunned. God talks to people that routinely? I learned that He most certainly does when He said to me, "I want you to pray like Rosemary is praying." I couldn't say no.

I was obedient to put His kingdom first and began to pray regularly, and as a reward, God gave me my life back. It wasn't long after that when I felt a tap on the shoulder one Sunday morning before church and turned to see a man holding out a guitar. "God told me to give you this," he said. With my surrender, everything that had been lost was restored. During that season of regeneration, everything flowed like oil from a rock. Whenever I opened the Bible, it was like seeing the words for the first time, and I was given revelation upon revelation, many of which I'm sharing for the first time here. If I was curious about something or felt uninformed, I would say, "What about this?" God would answer, "Let me tell you about that." It was a precious time.

So, here we are, Paul Ige Adeyanju and I, sharing what we've learned, and I'm honored to collaborate with such an expressive man. We've both come to this conclusion: God is still speaking new things. For instance, I've often wondered why the armies that surround Jerusalem in the books of Ezekiel and Revelation consist of riders on horseback. We live in an age where aircraft, ships, tanks, and drones do all the destroying, not knights on horses. What's going on?

I asked God about this, and here's what He showed me: When Jesus returns, the devil will be cast into a pit for 1,000 years, a period known as "The Millennium," and the *Age of Peace* will begin. There has been none like it in all of history. During the *Age of Peace*, weapons of every type will be disassembled and repurposed, armies will be discharged permanently, and nations will "never again learn how to make war." (Isaiah 2:4) Even the animal kingdom will be released from its fear. "An infant will play by a Cobra's den." (Isaiah 11:8)

When the devil is ultimately released, there won't even be a shotgun on the planet. When he incites some of the population to turn against Jesus, they will ride off to their destruction on horseback. No doubt whatever has replaced cars and trucks will come into play, but the idea is clear—the citizens of earth won't know how to make war anymore. It's a riveting adventure story, and true. I hope the future excites you. I hope this book inspires you to converse with God for yourself. He's waiting. Nothing going on outside your door is taking Him by surprise and He would like to talk to you about it personally. The King's wisdom is free for the asking.

- **Greg Mann**

About The King's Wisdom

DEVOTIONALS COME IN ALL SHAPES AND SIZES, like an assortment of tools in a carpenter's workshop. Some are prescriptive, designed to give you the precise measurements, a blueprint for how to live according to biblical principles. They're like the voice of the Apostle Paul, calling out commands to the early churches: Pray. Repent. Live in a way that honors God. Practical advice for the trenches of life, much like Ephesians 5:1-2—straightforward, no-nonsense instructions on what it means to live a life set apart.

These devotionals don't leave room for ambiguity. They get down to business, showing you the path and daring you to walk it. They're the kind of words that slice through the fog of confusion, like a beam of light cutting through the dark. No matter how complicated life may seem, these devotionals say, "This is the way—walk in it."

There are also some that are reflective. These are quieter. They don't call out commands. They're not about telling you what to do, but about helping you see what's already there. These devotionals encourage you to pause, to take a long look in the mirror of Scripture and see what's staring back at you. They invite you to sit in the stillness and wrestle with the deep questions, the ones that don't have easy answers.

It's like David in the Psalms, sitting under a starry sky, pondering the greatness of God: "Search me, O God, and know my heart; try me, and know my thoughts" (Psalm 139:23, 24). Reflective devotionals don't push you to act—they pull you into the heart of the Father, into a deeper communion that can only be found in the quiet places. They're the kind of words that sink into your soul like rain into parched soil.

This book, *The King's Wisdom*, is a blend of both. There will be moments when you'll feel like you're being handed a set of instructions, a map to guide you through the rough terrain of life. And then there will be times when you're simply invited to sit and reflect, to allow the weight of God's presence to settle over you like a warm blanket on a cold night.

As you make your way through these pages, we hope that you'll encounter God's wisdom in ways you never have before. Where there's been confusion, His clarity will shine through like the first light of dawn. Where you've felt weak, His strength will rise within you like a tidal wave. And where despair has taken root, His encouragement will uproot it, making room for hope to grow.

The world is moving faster than ever. Change is the only constant, and stability often feels like a distant memory. But amidst all the chaos, one thing stands unshaken: the word of God. "Heaven and earth will pass away, but My words will never pass away." (Matthew 24:35) That's the anchor, the solid rock that's been guiding God's people for millennia, from the days of David and Solomon to the present.

So, open your heart, prepare your mind, and let the King's wisdom speak. Don't just read these words—receive them. Let them sink into your bones, take root in your spirit. We pray that these words will be like seeds, planted in the fertile soil of your soul, ready to bear fruit that will last long after this book is closed and shelved.

Divine Purpose, Identity, and Calling

The believer's journey begins with discovering who we are in Christ and understanding our divine calling.

A Divine Collaboration

See, I have chosen Bezalel son of Uri, the son of Hur, of the tribe of Judah, and I have filled him with the Spirit of God, with wisdom, with understanding, with knowledge and with all kinds of skills — to make artistic designs for work in gold, silver, and bronze, to cut and set stones, to work in wood, and to engage in all kinds of crafts.

Exodus 31:2-4

Picture an artist standing before a blank canvas, brush in hand, ready to create. In the quiet of that moment, something stirs deep within, sparking a vision that transcends the ordinary. As the brush meets the canvas, colors swirl, shapes emerge, and a masterpiece begins to unfold. This isn't just creativity—it's communion with the Divine. Creation itself speaks to God's intricate design. From the galaxies above to the tiniest atom, His handiwork is everywhere. But in all this vastness, human beings hold a unique place.

Consider Bezalel, the artist chosen by God in Exodus 31:2-4 to oversee the artistic needs of the tabernacle in the wilderness and its priests. He didn't first turn to a prophet like Moses, but instead selected Bezalel, a humble and hitherto unknown man, and filled him with His Spirit—the first recorded instance of this in Scripture. Bezalel's task was to transform simple materials into stunning, eye-catching objects that would reflect God's glory.

What's remarkable here isn't just Bezalel's skill. It's the collaboration between Creator and creation. God didn't just hand Bezalel a blueprint—He invited him to join in the creative process. This partnership turned ordinary craftsmanship into a sacred act of worship. And that's the key. Creativity can become more than a mere hobby; it can become a divine calling. Through art, music, writing, or any other form of expression, we can illuminate darkness, inspire the weary, and reveal God's love. Every brushstroke, every note, every word has the potential to carry the presence of God, transforming the mundane into the magnificent.

Ephesians 2:10 reminds us, "For we are God's handiwork, created in Christ Jesus to do good works, which God prepared in advance for us to do." Like Bezalel, we're all called to bring our gifts to God and allow His Spirit to guide and inspire our work. When our creativity aligns with His vision, we become part of something far greater—a masterpiece that reflects His glory. So, the next time you pick up a paintbrush, pen, or instrument, remember that you're not just creating; you're worshiping. You're collaborating with the Creator Himself, contributing to the beauty and truth that showcase His greatness to the world. In His grand design, you are a unique brushstroke, and the world is waiting for your masterpiece.

Cleansed, Called, Commissioned

Then one of the seraphim flew to me with a live coal in his hand, which he had taken with tongs from the altar. 7 With it he touched my mouth and said, "See, this has touched your lips; your guilt is taken away and your sin atoned for.

Isaiah 6:6,7

Growing up in Nigeria, I was a bookworm who loved to sing and write poetry. I was also the handy guy in the family who repaired things that broke. The satellite dish, the radio, the TV—you name it, it was my duty to fix it. But aptitude doesn't always point to a calling. At around thirteen or so, when the younger kids in the neighborhood were let out of school for the holidays, I would gather them together and teach them math. After two weeks, I would give them their final exams and hold a makeshift award ceremony. The best pupils received certificates of completion. I didn't know it, but this was God preparing me for my future. I enjoy other things—art, music, and writing in particular, but my primary calling is to be a teacher and, potentially, an entrepreneur.

In the cryptic book of Isaiah, chapter 6, a vision unfolds that speaks of divine callings. In Isaiah's encounter with God, his subsequent response serves as a haunting reminder of our own urgent need to step into our purpose. In the vision, Isaiah is transported to the celestial throne room where he is surrounded by the glory of the Almighty. Standing in the presence of God, he is immediately confronted by his own sinfulness and that of his people. He cries out in anguish, "Woe to me! I am ruined! For I am a man of unclean lips, and I live among a people of unclean lips, and my eyes have seen the King, the Lord Almighty." His confession mirrors the despair that sin brings, a heavy burden that seems impossible to lift. But then, from the divine altar, an angelic being flies to Isaiah carrying a live coal. Touching it to Isaiah's lips, the seraphim declares, "See, this has touched your lips; your guilt is taken away and your sin atoned for."

This purification is something Isaiah could never have achieved on his own. It's a divine intervention, a celestial reset button that marks the beginning of his prophetic walk. When God asks, "Whom shall I send? And who will go for us?" Isaiah responds with a courageous, "Here am I. Send me!" He accepts the daunting mission to deliver a message to a people destined to hear but never understand.

Now that you have been saved, redeemed, and freed from sin, what will you do with that freedom? Will you answer the call of God? Isaiah stepped forward in faith, despite the odds stacked against him. We, too, are summoned to be God's messengers in a world that often resists the truth. The urgency for sinners to repent, and for believers to step up, is more pressing than ever. Time is fleeting, and the opportunity for redemption is now. Be bold in your repentance and fervent in your calling. The world needs witnesses to the transformative power of God's love. Will you be that witness? "The harvest is plentiful, but the workers are few. Ask the Lord of the harvest, therefore, to send out workers into his harvest field." (Matthew 9:37, 38) Step into the field, answer the call, and become the witness God has called you to be. The world is waiting.

Preserved For a Purpose

For He will command His angels concerning you to guard you in all your ways.

Psalm 91:11

When Jesus saved us, He did not transport us immediately to heaven. If that were the sole objective, we would have been taken up the moment we believed. However, God has a far greater plan in mind — one that involves a unique purpose for each of our lives. In His infinite wisdom and mercy, He preserves us so that we may fulfill the destiny He has designed for us. His protection, guidance, and preservation are not aimed at making life simple or free of hardship, but rather to ensure we walk fully in the purpose He has ordained. Jesus Himself faced immense difficulties during His earthly life, and His disciples, including Peter, encountered numerous setbacks. We are not exempt from these struggles. Yet, in every trial, every fall, God's hand is constantly at work to lift us up and keep us moving forward. "Though the righteous fall seven times, they rise again." (Proverbs 24:16)

Growing up in a Christian family in Nigeria, I witnessed firsthand the reality of spiritual warfare. Spiritual battles were not an abstract concept; they were an integral part of life. Our home was a place of constant prayer and spiritual resilience.

When I was thirteen, I experienced a spiritual attack that left a profound impact on my life. One evening during a storm, I was struck by lightning while standing in the kitchen next to a window. The next thing I knew, I was in the living room with a plate in my hand, unharmed but dazed, and unable to speak for a moment. When I told my mother what had happened, she simply nodded, acknowledging the seriousness of the event, then encouraged me to either eat or join her in prayer.

Later that evening, my twin brother told me of a similarly shocking experience. While at a friend's house, he narrowly avoided being struck by lightning when it hit his friend. This occurred at the exact same time I was struck. The devil was trying to destroy both my brother and me, but prayer protected us. My mother, in her matter of fact way, explained that she had been prompted to pray for both of us at the very moment those events were unfolding.

This was not the only time my family encountered such spiritual events, but in this instance, I was directly in the crosshairs. When I was a few months old, a prophecy concerning me was given to my mom, that my twin brother and I would one day lift our family out of poverty. At five years, I received another prophecy—that I would speak in front of many people in foreign lands. My mother often reminds us of these prophecies, and of the lightning strikes that were a deliberate attack on the destiny that had been spoken over our lives.

The enemy was trying to derail us, but God's preserving hand prevailed. "For He will command His angels concerning you to guard you in all your ways." (Psalm 91:11) God's divine protection is not merely a comforting thought but a spiritual truth. The challenges we face are often an indication that we are walking toward a greater purpose, one worth defending. He will preserve us through every storm, every setback, and every attack to ensure that His plans come to fruition. And we know that "all things work for the good of those who love Him, who have been called according to His purpose." (Romans 8:28) God's hand is always upon us to ensure that nothing can thwart the destiny He has placed before us.

Kings and Priests

*To Him who loved us and washed us from our sins in His own blood, and has made us
kings and priests to His God and Father…*

Revelation 1:5,6

In Old Testament times, beginning with King Saul and his replacement
King David, the people of Israel were classified as either laymen,
priests, or kings. In New Testament times, which include the present
day, the three have become one in every believer. "With Your blood
you purchased for God persons from every tribe and language and
people and nation and have made us kings and priests to our God. And
we will reign on the earth." (Revelation 5:9, 10) The "king" part is fairly
easy to understand. We know that we are "seated with Jesus in heavenly
places" (Ephesians 2:6), and have been given authority to cast out
demons and bind the powers of darkness. But what about the "priest"
part? What does that entail?

The first thing that comes to mind is worship, because we associate
priests with church, singing, and altars, but everybody in Israel was
expected to participate in expressions of worship from the king to the
layman. So, what then? What is God telling us when he calls us priests?
He is telling us that the waters that stretch out to block our way will
now part for us. Beginning with Moses, wherever the Israelites went,
no barrier could block them as long as the priests went first. The Red
Sea parted for Moses, the Jordan River parted for the priests who
carried the ark of the covenant, and Elijah and Elisha were able to
divide the river with a strike of their cloak. Jesus himself showed his
mastery of blockage when he walked across the storm-tossed Sea of
Galilee as easily as crossing on a bridge.

The ultimate blockage, of course, was when the veil that separated man from God and Jesus, our High Priest, opened up for us, giving us direct access to the throne. The idea is still the same in the present day. A blockage cannot withstand a priest. It cannot withstand you! It will require stepping up to and into; but power will go forth the very moment your feet meet the boundaries of the water. Immediately, God's power against obstacles is loosed on your behalf. You cannot fail except through disobedience or turning back. You have the assurance that circumstances will yield to you as long as God has led you to them. To that end, stay in prayer. Don't move until the word comes to do so. When the Word does come, step out immediately knowing that there is not a barrier on earth that can keep God from His purposes, and you are going specifically at His directive, a priest on assignment.

Your Newborn Voice

Now go; I will help you speak and will teach you what to say.

Exodus 4:11,12

When my son was born, his entry into the world came with a universal cry. The sound was so primal it sent shivers down my spine. It was more than just a wail of discomfort, it was a declaration, an announcement that he had arrived. A baby's cry isn't just noise, it's the first note in the symphony of life, a voice that's meant to grow, evolve, and never be silenced. There are plenty of theories about why newborns cry when they first breathe the air of this world. Some say it's the pressure—the squeezing of that fragile skull and the shock of leaving the womb's warmth for the cold, bright chaos outside.

Whatever the reason, that cry is a milestone. "I am here." That voice, small and new, is both literal and symbolic, the beginning of communication and the first sign of individuality. As days turn into months, a baby's voice doesn't stay the same. It morphs, shifts, learns, and adapts. First, there's babbling, then screaming, all of it a child's way of pushing their vocal cords to the limit. They don't need to understand language to know that their voice holds power—it's an innate truth they carry within. But here's the thing about life. It has a way of dulling that sharp, clear voice we're born with.

As we grow, the world piles on its expectations and insists that we conform, quiet down, and blend in. The voice that once rang out with boldness starts to waver, softened by the weight of judgment and doubt. Slowly, we lose faith in our voice, forgetting the power it holds. Jesus foresaw this when He said in Matthew 18:3: "Truly I tell you, unless you change and become like little children, you will never enter the kingdom of heaven." This has to do primarily with purity and faith, but it's also a call to reclaim the uninhibited nature of a child's voice.

Consider Moses. He wasn't sure he was the guy for the job, as he doubted his ability to speak on God's behalf. "Pardon your servant, Lord. I have never been eloquent, neither in the past nor since you have spoken to your servant. I am slow of speech and tongue," he says in Exodus 4:10. But God's response is direct, "Who gave human beings their mouths? Now go; I will help you speak and will teach you what to say." (Exodus 4:11, 12)

Moses learned that his voice, flawed as it seemed, was powerful when backed by God. It could challenge empires and part seas. Our voices can as well. In Proverbs 31:8,9 we're commanded to, "Speak up for those who cannot speak for themselves, for the rights of all who are destitute. Speak up and judge fairly; defend the rights of the poor and needy." Your voice isn't just for you— it's a tool meant to cut through the noise, to speak the truth and bring justice. The enemy will try to silence you, but your voice is meant to shake the foundations of darkness.

From that first cry at birth to the fully realized voice of adulthood, the journey is one of growth, discovery, and often, reclamation. Whether you're raising your voice against injustice, expressing truths through song or writing, or simply bringing light to someone's day, don't let anything or anyone silence you. Find your voice and reclaim it. Let it ring out loud and clear for the glory of God.

Profound Activation

Blessed is she who believed, for there will be a fulfillment of all the things which were told her by the Lord.

Luke 1:45

An explosive activation occurs when you say yes to a word from God in the very moment that it arrives. Spiritual conception occurs, and something that hasn't previously existed in the natural world is now on its way to becoming.

The lapse between conception and manifestation varies—it could be long or short depending on God's timing—but the idea is similar to that of pregnancy. In fact, the process of birthing by faith shares the same power as the enigma described by Paul in Ephesians 5:31,32 concerning a marriage covenant: "The two shall become one flesh. This is a great mystery." The "two becoming one" in a faith action refers to GOD AS THE PROMISER and you as THE RECEIVER OF THE PROMISE.

In the case with Mary in the book of Luke, the angel Gabriel told her that the Holy Spirit would overshadow her, causing her to conceive a son. This was God declaring something and Mary responded without hesitation: "Let it be done to me according to your word." (Luke 1:38) Immediately, the creative spark that had been lingering over her life leaped alive into the closed circuit of covenant believing.

There is a fact to be understood here. The power of conceiving by faith is so effectual that follow-up rituals are unnecessary. In word-of-faith circles we are taught to confess scriptures over our lives, an absolutely beautiful practice, but in the case of a received covenant promise nothing more needs to be done. In Mary's case, she didn't have to repeat "I'm going to have a baby in Jesus' name" for the next nine months of her pregnancy to ensure that the desired outcome would come to pass. She could have, but the desired outcome was not dependent on her institution of a habit. All Mary (and Joseph) had to do was live Godly and obey the instructions of the Lord until the child was born.

The same principle of faith applies to all of God's promises. Whether they come as a Rhema word from God, or you discover them for yourself in the Bible, if you believe them and say yes to them by faith, you can have them. There is nothing as wonderful as the feeling you'll get when your faith snaps like a magnet to God's ability. Gears drop into place and the energy of spiritual power begins to churn, making it impossible to doubt in that moment. If you are operating in hope only, and not true faith, you'll know it. Conception won't occur. The solution? Spend more time with God, the lover of your soul, by making His word your bread. And through that intimacy, faith for anything will come.

I want to remind you again that faith just requires one instance of genuine believing. Repetition is not necessary, except to guard your mouth and "hold fast to the confession of your faith without wavering, for He who promised is faithful." (Hebrews 10:23) Don't speak doubting words that run contrary to what God originally said to you. And know that He is still speaking to you even now, saying, "Shall I bring to the time of birth and not also cause the delivery?" (Isaiah 66:9) Your promise is on its way.

Recognition

The work is great and extensive, and we are spread out far from one another along the wall. Wherever you hear the sound of the horn, rally to us there. Our God will fight for us!

Nehemiah 4:19-20

Kingdom work is not a small thing but is "great and extensive." (Nehemiah 4:19) It takes the entire body of Christ to do it. The visible parts (eyes, ears, fingers and legs) and the invisible parts (internal organs, white blood cells and the electricity of the nervous system), all have a part to play. If we could see ourselves from space, we might become disheartened. Looking down, we would observe that the Body of Christ is scattered across all of the continents of the earth and are "separated far from one another on the wall." (Nehemiah 4:19) There are many gaps between our members, and there is a lot of restless and perhaps unnecessary movement taking place. The church is fidgety. But if we are really serious about kingdom work, we can't just say, "I'm going to live here," or "I'm going to go live there," without checking in through prayer and expect to get the job done properly. It takes two hands to hold a plow, not an ear and a hand; and we aren't the ones who decide who is what and how we are connected to so-and-so and in what way. We must let God arrange everything. To be sure, we have free will and can do as we please, but *wisdom* has a sister named *recognition* and it is through her eyes and ears that we'll find ourselves properly positioned.

Recognition is the battle horn that trumpets loudly to indicate where we are to take our stand. Recognition told Jesus that it was time to leave a line of sick people and say to his disciples "We must go on to the next town." Recognition made the baby in Elizabeth's belly leap for joy upon hearing the voice of Mary, because of the child she carried. Recognition moved the disciples in Jerusalem to extend the right hand of fellowship to Paul and Barnabas, two wild roamers whom they'd only heard rumors about. Recognition, not intuition or goosebumps. Forget following feelings, there's too much at stake. Having the right people alongside us—individuals of like and precious faith—is important because random combinations won't produce the right result.

So, what do we do? If the trumpet of recognition isn't currently sounding, we wait. It will come. And then, "Wherever you hear the sound of the trumpet, rally there." (Nehemiah 4:20) The Holy Spirit is the trumpeter. He will make it very plain to you what to do, who to join up with, who to start a business or ministry with, and even who to marry.

Be confident that the clear indicators of the Holy Spirit are of a higher pitch than any emotional noises in your life and any warfare you might currently be experiencing. You will hear Him. There might be fog to the left and fog to the right but down the center is, clarity. "You will hear a voice behind you saying, 'this is the way, walk in it,' when you veer to the right hand or the left." (Isaiah 30:21) If you let God do all of your arranging for you, your recognition will become sharpened by experience to the point where you will never again doubt your ability to discern His will. And then, best of all, because you have rallied to the right place on the wall, God will fight for you, and He is not about to be defeated. Blessings will encompass your family, your work and all of your relationships and the purposes of God will continue to advance in every aspect of your life.

The First Valley
(The Valley of Childhood)

While his parents were returning home, the boy Jesus stayed behind in Jerusalem.

Luke 2:43

Childhood is as fleeting as the hours of dawn. An event unique to this present creation. There were no children before the earth existed and there will be none afterwards. We all experience the same exciting, but molasses-slow drift, through the fog of our earliest years. During that time, we are potter's clay in the mixing stage. The new life is still getting used to breathing, crawling, walking and running, and the shadows that hover at the perimeter—God and the devil—mostly just watch at first. Even the events of Jesus' life from zero to twelve years remain a mystery. The information is private. For a while at least, the family was allowed to live as other families did.

A child's life from zero to five years has mostly to do with bonding and the expansion of the senses—a gentle, upward slope. A life laid out on a graph reveals that a valley forms between the ages of five and twelve. This is "*The Valley of Right and Wrong*," and critical lessons are learned there. There is a valley for adults too—the "*Valley of Decision*" mentioned in Joel 3:14. But "*The Valley of Right and Wrong*" must be traversed first. A child must learn to distinguish the truth from a lie.

During this period, two spiritual fathers are at war to try to establish paternity: our Heavenly Father and the father of lies. Both will present themselves in unique ways, specific to the nature and spirit of the child in question, with the devil doing more probing and prying (to pinpoint strengths and weaknesses early on), and God doing a great deal of loving exposition. I myself was a good example that "foolishness is bound up in the heart of a child." (Proverbs 22:15) I was a Jacob, a master manipulator, and was always trying to supplant my siblings. I was sneaky. At the ripe old age of six, God saw the character flaw (that takes maintenance to this day) and came down to stand in my way, and here is how that occurred:

One Saturday morning I was fighting with one of my brothers about who would get the prize in a cereal box. I knew it was his turn, but I refused to relent, sending him running in tears to complain to our father. Quickly, I dug the prize out and stuffed it deep into my pajama pocket. Aha! I won again. However, God had a different outcome in mind. To my astonishment, when my brother returned, he reached into the same cereal box and pulled out an exact duplicate of the prize I was hiding in my pocket! "Dad said it was my turn," he exclaimed, waving his trophy proudly.

It was a miracle. My family was not a Christian family, but in that moment, I knew that God was real. He made sure of it. I felt both His love and discipline at the same time and knew that unjust scales would not be tolerated. It was a deep lesson for a six-year-old. I would go on to lie, steal and cheat again, of course, but I would never be able to claim ignorance. I had eaten from the forbidden fruit in *"The Valley of Right and Wrong"* and knew that someone was watching. Someone that loved me very much but for my own sake wouldn't let me sin without consequence. That's what love is. A constant steering away from darkness. He has never let go of my hand.

It's Time to See

Faith is the substance of things hoped for, the evidence of things not seen.

Hebrews 11:1

When I turned thirteen, something changed. I wouldn't call myself a recluse, but I found myself drawn to solitude like never before. It wasn't that I didn't have friends—I did, plenty of them. We'd hang out, play football (soccer), and do the usual teenage things, but when I got home, I craved something else, something quieter. I'd lock myself in my room, open the book of Proverbs, and dive into its ancient wisdom. Day after day, I'd pick up where I left off, the words sinking deeper into my soul. It wasn't long before I found poetry. Or maybe it found me. The rhythm of words, the way they could capture a fleeting thought and pin it down on paper—it was like magic. Poetry became my outlet, my way of making sense of the swirling thoughts that stayed buried in my mind. But then, when I turned eighteen, something happened that would change everything.

I woke up one morning with a phrase echoing in my head: "It's time to see." It was like a whisper from somewhere deep inside, a call to open my eyes to something beyond the ordinary. And so I did what I always did—I grabbed a pen and began to write. The words flowed out of me, a poem that seemed to come from somewhere beyond my understanding.

I can see the blind see,
I can hear the dumb speak,
I can feel the deaf hear,
I now know the dullards can imagine.
I have eyes, so I can see,

I envisage the vision of a productive tomorrow,
I have ears, so I can hear.
I can hear babies crying to be cared for,
I can hear songs of victory filling the atmosphere.
I can see trifles becoming valuables.

It was a strange poem, a mix of paradox and possibility, but it carried a truth that I couldn't shake. It was time to see. Not just with my physical eyes, but with the eye of the Spirit. And trust me, it's as real as the nose on your face. A few months later, I found myself on a plane headed to Miami, Florida. The poem, the phrase, the whole experience—it all made sense in a way that I couldn't have predicted. Since that flight, I've been living in the United States and the rest, as they say, is history.

The first step in the walk of faith is to see. Not with the eyes that scan the world around us, but with the eyes of the Spirit. Hebrews 11:1 says, "Faith is the substance of things hoped for, the evidence of things not seen." Think about that for a second—substance is evidence. In the realm of faith, substance is tied to the things we can't see with our natural eyes. Then, using faith, we reach into the unseen realm and pull God's promises into reality.

It's not voodoo or black magic. It's scriptural, spiritual, and powerful. But here's the catch: once we see with the eyes of the Spirit, we've got to align our actions and feelings with that vision. Feelings can be slippery; they're fickle, flimsy, and extremely ephemeral. They lead us around like blind men, stumbling through life without direction. We have to determine that we are no longer going to be tossed around by the waves of emotion. And that, my friend, is where true power lies.

So, the next time you find yourself overwhelmed by what you see with your natural eyes, remember to stop trusting them to guide you spiritually. Use the eyes of the Spirit. Let the spirit man inside you have dominance over the natural man. That's where faith begins and where real life truly takes shape.

The Wayward Body

Proverbs 18:16

I share the following without judgment because I've been guilty of presumptuous error myself at times.

I knew a woman once who was fixed on being successful in business, but every time she stood up to teach or preach, the anointing fell upon her. Meanwhile, her business ventures never took off. I knew a successful businessman who decided to start a Church but his very first message had all the power of dust settling. He was not called to preach or pastor. Eventually, he and his wife lost their house and business trying to keep their floundering church afloat. It was sad to see. I knew a woman in the helps ministries who desperately wanted to be the prophetess of her church, but when her every word was not heeded to, she became offended and left the church altogether. I knew a gifted worship leader once who desired fame and fortune, but the calling wasn't there, and the doors never opened.

Conversely, I have known highly gifted musicians who were called to worldwide influence, but they were afraid to leave the stages of their churches. I have seen prophets try to be playwrights, intercessors try to be singers, artists try to be filmmakers, entertainers try to be preachers, pastors try to be insurance salesmen, guitar players try to be teachers, and piano players try to be catalog models. I have known all of these personally. I ran into a successful salesman once who decided he wanted to be a TV evangelist, and although he was able to sell himself to backers, cameras didn't love him and caused him to freeze up and act unnaturally. His anointing left.

What is all this? Part of it is spiritual warfare and part of it is the flesh. Part of it is right, but part of it isn't. We are taught to *"possess the land"* as the Israelites did and be brave and *"press toward the goal for the prize of the high calling,*" but the devil likes to channel this noble zeal into false directions that do nothing but wear us down. This is a beguiling of sorts, and it begins with the simplest and most below-the-surface type of malaise--dissatisfaction. We find ourselves thinking, "This isn't enough for me anymore. I'm created for better things because I'm a child of God and He will bless anything I do." Then, when we move into an area we're not called to, the devil lifts the everyday resistance that we experience as Christians and suddenly we feel like we're free and heading toward glory. A little success here, a small victory there— we are rewarded with a false sense of progress and achievement, but the feeling won't last for very long. Nor will there be any long-term fruit or profit. We are trying to do somebody else's job.

Have you heard the story about the accountant? His friends were always pressuring him to go on missionary trips with them, but he could not drum up the enthusiasm for it. However, when he would balance his customer's books and find the single missing penny, the anointing would fall. Like the accountant, you and I have an assignment that invites the anointing. We can teach ourselves to do a dozen things— fix cars, bake a cake, hem a dress, play a song on the piano, but to which of these should we devote most of our life? Our calling, of course!

How do we identify our calling? God gives us the clearest clue to this in Proverbs 18:16: "A man's gift opens doors for him." Each of us has a gift that, when we operate in it, doors open that don't for the others. It's that simple. When a gift continues to take you places, I would suggest that you stay on that path. When a gift consistently leads you to a dead end, no matter how enthusiastic you feel about it, I would suggest that you stop and fast and pray immediately. Continuing down false paths can prove costly.

Stepping into the unknown is part of our faith walk and there is no experience as exciting as walking "the high hills of the earth" with God, as long as He is the one guiding us. I knew a pastor once who liked to say, "God guides us, but the devil drives us." It's true. If you feel guided, you will find that it's absolutely possible to relax in green pastures and scale the heights of mountains at the same time. If you feel driven, running on impulse, turn around. The right doors are waiting for your gift to open them.

Your Pasts

(Your Dead Past and Your Prophetic Past)

Forget the former things; do not dwell on the past. See, I am doing a new thing! Now it springs up; do you not perceive it? I am making a way in the wilderness and streams in the wasteland.

Isaiah 43:18,19

We all carry two kinds of pasts with us: our dead past and our prophetic past. The dead past is a graveyard of our mistakes and regrets, a shadowy realm of *what ifs* and *if onlys*. When we visit it, we are recalling the good old days, a perilous quicksand that can trap us in a cycle of stagnation. The Bible cautions against this kind of nostalgia because it hinders us from fully serving God by keeping our mind trapped in reverie. Jesus' words in Luke 9:62 ring clear: "No one who puts his hand to the plow and looks back is fit for service in the kingdom of God."

In stark contrast, our prophetic past is a beacon of hope and direction. It consists of the promises and prophecies God has spoken over our lives, divine words meant to guide and encourage us. The Bible instructs us to cling to these promises and wield them like weapons in our spiritual battles. Paul's charge to Timothy in 1 Timothy 1:18 echoes this sentiment: "This command I entrust to you, Timothy, my son, in accordance with the prophecies previously made concerning you, that by them you fight the good fight." The devil revels in dragging us back into our dead past, making us wallow in self-pity and doubt, whispering that forward motion is futile. But God beckons us to focus on our prophetic past, His promises that light our path with hope and faith.

Consider Abraham, who, despite his old age, held on to God's promise of countless descendants. It took twenty-five years, but the promise began to manifest with the birth of his son Isaac. Or take

Joseph, whose dreams foretold of his future greatness. Despite being sold into slavery and thrown into prison, Joseph held fast to God's promise. In time, he rose to prominence in Egypt, just as God had foretold. Psalm 105:19 recounts his journey: "Until the time that his word came to pass, the word of the LORD tested him."

You must resist the pull of your dead past and instead focus on the promises given to you. Nostalgia is a dead tomb. The songs of your youth were for then, not now. Don't recall them, sing them, draw inspiration from them or pass them along to the next generation. Instead, trust in God's future and stride forward with conviction, knowing that He has a plan for your life and is able to bring that plan to fruition.

Let the words of Isaiah 43:18,19 be your anthem: "Forget the former things; do not dwell on the past. See, I am doing a new thing! Now it springs up; do you not perceive it? I am making a way in the wilderness and streams in the wasteland." We all have two pasts, our dead past and our prophetic past, but only one connects with your future. Hold fast to those prophecies made concerning you.

Battles and Spiritual Warfare

After understanding our calling, we often face spiritual battles. Confronting and overcoming spiritual opposition early on in the faith journey is inevitable.

A Troublesome Scripture

Unless the Lord builds the house, they labor in vain who build.
Psalm 127:1

A pastor friend of mine declared to me recently that the scariest passage in the Bible is Psalm 127:1. "Unless the Lord builds the house, they labor in vain who build." It's true. Time is the only thing that can't be restored when it's lost, so when we waste time and vitality on something that God has not sanctioned, there is no redeeming it.

Years ago, I got into a relationship with a woman who lived in another state, and we decided to marry. We seemed like an ideal match—we were both on worship teams and were spirit-filled and shared the same life goals, but for reasons unknown to us, God was strictly against it. He let us both know early on that we needed to lay the relationship down and move on. In fact, on the very same Wednesday evening, a prophet called her forward in her church in Iowa and told her she that was involved in a wrong relationship while I received the same message from the Holy Spirit in my church in Oklahoma. But we persisted anyway, holding on to the belief that once we were married, our relationship would become God's will even if it hadn't been before. What a presumptuous idea that is, to think that we can change God's will by forcing His hand. Don't test Him that way.

Two weeks before the wedding, I was checking the mail with my two young daughters from a previous marriage when one of them looked up at me and blurted out, "Unless the Lord builds the house, they labor in vain who build!" It came gushing forth, followed by wide eyes and a perplexed look, as she didn't have any clue as to the foreboding, prophetic weight of the words she had just uttered. This was God's final warning to me, "I'm not with you." Needless to say, the marriage was a complete disaster. It was beset with chaos, confusion, strife and fruitlessness, and only the pain of another divorce could set things right again. That was a hard lesson, but I learned it. If God is not our partner in our marriages, businesses, and ministries, they will fail. God is a loving Father who is very involved in the details of His children's lives and His tapestries of connectivity are not to be tampered with. He knows what He's doing.

Psalm 127:1 also reveals a further truth: "Unless the Lord guards the city, the watchman stays awake in vain." The watchman symbolizes prayer, revealing to us that any prayer dedicated to changing a situation God doesn't want changed is wasted effort. I can attest to that. During my marriage to that woman, we had the congregations of two separate, faith-filled churches praying for us to no avail. Imagine that! Useless prayer. It does exist.

Always consult with God when it comes to partnerships and relationships. If you do, your prayers are guaranteed to be effective. None will fall flat. Everything will work because your foundation is in Jesus and not a flood, storm or contrary word can tear it down.

Dragons and Treasures 1
(Discouragement)

But those who hope in the Lord will renew their strength.
They will soar on wings like eagles.
Isaiah 40:31

In the quiet, lonely moments of our life's journey, a dragon awaits to seep into our hearts like a slow poison, draining us of hope and vigor. This is the *dragon of discouragement.*

Discouragement is a stealthy adversary, creeping in when we're tired, overwhelmed, and on the brink of despair. It tells us that our efforts are in vain and that our struggles will never end. It tells us that giving up is easier than pressing on. But Isaiah 40:31 offers us this hopeful message: "Those who wait upon the Lord will renew their strength. They will soar on wings like eagles."

I'm naturally hyper-optimistic, so discouragement rarely gets the best of me. I've been tested, though. After moving to Tulsa, Oklahoma, for Bible school, I thought everything was finally on track. Then I got a message from my enrollment advisor that I was out of status on my visa and needed to apply for a reinstatement. Talk about a buzz kill. Returning to Nigeria would mean starting all over again.

I called my parents and told them, "If you don't see me back home soon, it means a miracle happened," and they ramped up their prayers. For a year and a half, I was stuck in limbo, living with friends and unable to work legally. My days were a blur of waking up, reading the Word of God and doing chores. For the first time, I understood what it felt like to be depressed. It was a challenging season, but I kept God at the center of things and eventually was reinstated, finished Bible school, and even graduated with a surplus of money in my school account.

Consider the prophet Elijah, who faced this same dragon of discouragement in his own wilderness. After a mighty victory against the prophets of Baal, he fled from Jezebel's wrath and found himself alone, exhausted, and begging for death under a broom tree. "I have had enough, Lord," he said. "Take my life; I am no better than my ancestors." (1 Kings 19:4) Yet, in his darkest hour, an angel touched him, providing food, water, and a reminder of God's presence. Renewed in body and spirit, Elijah was able to continue in his mission. We see here that even the mightiest heroes can falter, but God's provision is always there.

Charles Spurgeon, in his comforting work *"Morning and Evening,"* speaks to the heart of those battling discouragement. He reminds us that God's promises are the only antidote to despair, offering a wellspring of strength and hope. Spurgeon emphasizes that when we feel weak, God's strength is made perfect in our weakness.

Each moment we choose to hope, we pierce the dragon's hide and reclaim our treasure—renewed strength. Imagine the resilience that comes from this treasure. No longer do we stumble under the weight of our burdens. We soar, unburdened and free, carried by the strength that only God can provide, and are given bursts of energy that lift us up when we can no longer lift ourselves. So, cling to the promises of God, immerse yourself in His word, and seek His presence in prayer. Draw strength from the stories of those who have gone before us, like Elijah, who found renewal in his darkest hour. With each act of hope, each renewal of strength, you weaken the hold of the dragon of discouragement and move closer to the treasures of strength and perseverance that will sustain you through every trial and tribulation.

Dragons and Treasures 2
(Doubt)

But when you ask, you must believe and not doubt, because the one who doubts is like a wave of the sea, blown and tossed by the wind.
James 1:6

In the shadowy corners of our hearts, another dragon waits. This one doesn't roar or snarl, it whispers, planting seeds of uncertainty deep in our minds until they take root and grow into choking vines. This is the *dragon of doubt*. Doubt is a subtle serpent, wrapping itself around our thoughts, squeezing tight until every shred of confidence is drained. It tells us that we're incapable, and that we are adrift on a sea of inadequacies. James 1:6 describes this dragon's handiwork: "But when you ask, you must believe and not doubt because the one who doubts is like a wave of the sea, blown and tossed by the wind."

The story of Peter walking on water is often told, but its lessons are as deep as the sea. At Jesus' beckoning, Peter stepped out of the boat and onto the waves in a miracle of faith. His eyes were locked on Jesus, and he was walking on water until he glanced up at the storm and felt the wind, forcing him to cry out, "Lord, save me!" Jesus, with a touch of sadness, asked, "Why did you doubt?" (Matthew 14:22-33).

In his classic *My Utmost for His Highest*, Oswald Chambers dives into this very battle. Chambers speaks of the necessity of unwavering faith, the kind that stands firm even when the storm rages. He reminds us that doubt is not merely a lapse in belief, but a failure to trust the character and promises of God.

Back in 2016, God told me to go to Oral Roberts University, so with just $85 in my pocket, I took the plunge and enrolled. After the first semester, though, I found myself staring at a $4,000 bill. There I was, deep in the red, and my mind started spinning, wondering how I'd pay off that debt, let alone survive the next five semesters. But God made a way. Out of nowhere, someone I hadn't spoken to in two years connected me with his older brother, who then connected me to someone else who offered me an internship as a chaplain at a nonprofit. All of this happened over the course of a couple of weeks. Fast-forward to December of 2018, I graduated—debt-free.

This quick story is just a peek into how sneaky doubt can be. But it's also a reminder that God is a promise keeper, and when He says He'll do something, He absolutely will. Oh, and in that whirlwind of events? I met Greg, my co- author, through those relationships and eight years later, here we are!

Yes, the dragon of doubt is insidious, but a treasure lies just beyond it—steadfast faith. It is our beacon in the storm, not just nice to have but essential for a life lived boldly and purposefully. We all have our moments when doubt slithers in. Like Thomas, who needed to see and touch the wounds of Christ to believe, we sometimes falter. Jesus' response to Thomas is the same for us: "Blessed are those who have not seen and yet have believed." (John 20:29) Blessed, indeed, with the treasures of faith and assurance.

Just like the *dragon of discouragement*, the *dragon of doubt* is a formidable foe, but not an unconquerable one. With each act of trust, each step of faith, its grip is weakened, and we move closer to the treasures God has for us. Don't be like the waves, blown and tossed by the wind, but be a steadfast rock, anchored in the assurance of God's unchanging love and promises. By faith you can move mountains and weather any storm.

Dragons and Treasures 3
(Fear)

For God has not given us a spirit of fear, but of power and of love and of a sound mind.
2 Timothy 1:7

In the dimly lit corridors of our souls, lurking just beyond the edge of the light, there lies a beast many of us know all too well. This is the *dragon of fear*. Its gnawing, paralyzing force slinks into our lives quietly, starting as a whisper, and feeding on our doubts and insecurities. It grows stronger with every unchallenged thought. We are told in 2 Timothy 1:7, "For God has not given us a spirit of fear, but of power and of love and of a sound mind," yet it's still possible to find ourselves frozen in its grasp, unable to step out in faith.

Consider the story of Gideon. He was an ordinary man threshing wheat in a winepress, hiding from his enemies, when the Angel of the Lord appeared to him and called him a mighty warrior. Gideon's first reaction? Fear. He doubted his own strength, questioned God's choice, and demanded signs. So did Moses, Sarah, and many others. The angel's words to Gideon were clear: God had given him power. It took courage for Gideon to rise above his fear and lead an army of 300 men against a multitude, but his reward was victory over the Midianites, a renewed confidence, and legacy of faith.

One of my fiercest battles with fear came in 2011 after I moved from Nigeria to the U.S. to study. Financial troubles hit hard when my dad could no longer support my education. After a year and a half of hustling to keep my dreams alive, my school handed me an ultimatum: pay up or pack up. I faced the grim prospect of being kicked out, losing my international student status, and possibly being deported back to Nigeria. Fear loomed, but I clung to God's Word and prayer. Every day, three times a day, I'd head to a hidden spot under the stairs with my Bible and notebook, pouring out my heart in tears. Each time, I stood up not with answers, but with peace and strength to face whatever came next. The problem wasn't magically solved, and in fact, I did lose my student status for a while. But that's what led me to Tulsa, Oklahoma, where God's plan began to unfold in a dramatic way.

In the chaos of that season, those private moments with God gave me comfort and peace, and they shaped the rest of my life. When I finally left that school in Florida, fear no longer had a grip on me—I felt a calm assurance that God had something better. And He did!

I never dreamed of attending a school as prestigious (and pricey) as Oral Roberts University, but God's plans are bigger than ours. Fear had no chance against that. Max Lucado, in his book "Fearless," speaks to this very battle. He describes fear as a prison, chaining us to the mundane and keeping us from God's promises. Lucado argues that to live fearlessly is to live freely, embracing the power, love, and sound mind that God has given us. It's not about the absence of fear, but the presence of courage. Fear spews lies in the dark: "You're not enough. You will fail. Stay where it's safe." But these whispers are nothing compared to the roar of God's truth.

Like Gideon, we are called to face this dragon head on, armed with the knowledge that we are endowed with divine power. Each step we take in faith is a blow against the dragon, each act of courage is a strike that weakens its hold. Imagine the treasures that lie beyond this beast. The treasure of courage, a radiant gem, glittering with the light of a thousand victories. The treasure of confidence, a shield, forged in the fires of divine assurance, capable of withstanding the fiercest attacks. These are not mere trinkets; they are the keys to a life lived boldly, a life that echoes with the promises of God.

Remember that you are not alone in your battle. You have the power of God within you, and with each step of faith, you move closer to the treasure of a fearless heart. Even when your knees tremble, stand tall. Even when your heart races, step forward. The *dragon of fear* may be fearsome, but it is not invincible. And beyond it lies the treasure of a life lived in the full light of God's love and power.

Dragons and Treasures 4
(Pride)

Pride goes before destruction, a haughty spirit before a fall.
Proverbs 16:18

In the recesses of our hearts, hidden in the deepest, darkest corners, there slumbers a beast that all too often goes unnoticed until it's too late. This is the *dragon of pride*. Pride is a beast that wears many disguises. It purrs with satisfaction at our achievements, whispering that we are self-made, self-sufficient, and superior. It feeds our egos, bloating them until we can no longer see beyond ourselves. Proverbs 16:18 warns us with stark clarity: "Pride goes before destruction, a haughty spirit before a fall." This dragon thrives on our self-importance, leading us to believe that we stand alone at the top of the mountain, invulnerable, and untouchable.

Consider the story of King Nebuchadnezzar. He stood on the roof of his royal palace in Babylon and declared, "Is not this the great Babylon I have built as the royal residence, by my mighty power and for the glory of my majesty?" (Daniel 4:30) The dragon of pride had him in its grasp and his arrogance led to his downfall. Stripped of his sanity, for seven years he lived like an animal in the open fields until he acknowledged the sovereignty of God. Only then was his kingdom restored, and with it, the true treasure of humility. C. S. Lewis, in his seminal work *"Mere Christianity,"* delves deep into the dangers of pride. He describes it as the *great sin*, the root of all other sins. Pride, according to Lewis, is the complete anti-God state of mind.

During my time at Bible school, I worked as part of the custodial staff. Early on, we were told explicitly, "Do not drag stacked chairs across the floor. It leaves marks and looks terrible." Unfortunately, one evening in my first few months, that's exactly what I did. Then the next morning my boss called me into his office and escorted me to the room where I'd been working. The floor looked like a battlefield of scuff marks. He told me that the higher-ups wanted whoever did this to be fired. Then he asked why I didn't ask for help when I knew I couldn't lift the chairs alone. I fumbled through my words, admitting that I'd made a foolish mistake and deserved to be let go. I had no excuse. Then he hit me with a statement that shook me: "Paul, you have pride." I had never thought of myself as prideful, but he explained, "Pride is when you have a sincere need, but you can't bring yourself to ask for help." That definition stuck with me. I almost lost my job because of pride, but luckily, I kept it and ended up becoming one of my boss's top team members. We still keep in touch to this day.

Pride drops hints of lies in our ears: "You're better than them. You don't need help. You're the master of your fate." It blinds us to our weaknesses and inflates our self-worth to grotesque proportions, which can result in isolation, downfall, shame, and destruction. Yet, beyond the dragon of pride lies a treasure more precious than gold.

The treasure of humility is a gem that shines with the light of truth. It is the strength found in recognizing our need for God and others; the freedom in letting go of our inflated self-image. It allows us to stand firm in our identity as children of God, secure and grounded. Imagine the peace that comes from this treasure. No longer do we need to strive for self-importance or validation. We can rest in the knowledge that our worth is not tied to our achievements but to our relationship with God. The treasure of humility brings with it true strength, the kind that withstands any storm and resists any fall.

So, how do we confront this dragon? By remembering that every breath we take is a gift, not a right. By acknowledging our dependence on God and valuing the contributions of others. By looking to Jesus, who humbled Himself to serve and save humanity (Philippians 2:6-11).

Just like the dragons of fear and doubt, the *dragon of pride* is a formidable foe, but not an invincible one. With each act of humility, you weaken its grip and draw closer to the treasure that awaits you. Find strength and peace in humility. It is a treasure that enriches your life and aligns you with the heart of God.

Dragons and Treasures 5
(Temptation)

No temptation has overtaken you except what is common to mankind. And God is faithful; he will not let you be tempted beyond what you can bear.
1 Corinthians 10:13

Cloaked in the most alluring of disguises is the *dragon of temptation*. It beckons with a siren song, with an enchanting tune, offering delights that glisten and stimulate the senses.

Shortly after high school, I entered my first serious relationship. We spent a lot of time together watching movies, eating, and talking about the future. Both of us were serious about our walk with God, but when emotions are involved and you're alone for long stretches, temptation tends to show up uninvited. It started small—a peck on the cheek, and then a kiss—and soon we found ourselves going beyond innocent affection. One day, she invited me into her room to show me how organized she was, which led to making out on her bed. Suddenly, we both paused. Looking into each other's eyes, a question passed between us, "Are we really going to cross this line?" That's when I bolted out of the room like I'd been yanked up by the collar. She followed, both of us embarrassed and dazed like we'd seen a ghost. We had a serious conversation afterward and agreed to avoid situations where we'd be tempted like that again. I had made a covenant with God to save myself for marriage and wasn't willing to cross that line.

Later that night, while walking to the bus station, we passed a couple making out in the shadows against an unfinished fence, and I joked, "Look, they're having a Romans 2:1 moment"—a play on words, using *Romans* as a stand-in for *romance*. Curious, I pulled out my phone, looked up Romans 2:1, and read out loud. "Therefore, you have no excuse, you who pass judgment on someone else, for at whatever point you judge another, you are condemning yourself, because you who pass judgment do the same things." This struck us even harder. We were silent for the remainder of the walk to the bus station. When I got home, I cried, realizing how close I'd come to possibly derailing my life.

Temptation is a dragon that's hard to slay alone. You need God and a good support system to make it through. This dragon is a seducer, promising pleasure, power, and prestige, yet delivering only emptiness. It's the voice on the mountain offering all the kingdoms of the world, the glittering gold that distracts us from our true purpose (Matthew 4:1-11), and the forbidden fruit that seems so sweet (Genesis 3:1). But 1 Corinthians 10:13 offers a hand: "No temptation has overtaken you except what is common to mankind. And God is faithful; he will not let you be tempted beyond what you can bear."

Think of Jesus in the wilderness, facing the dragon of temptation head on. After forty days of fasting in the wilderness, He was weak, hungry, and vulnerable. The tempter came with three seductive offers: turn stones into bread, leap from the temple's pinnacle, and bow in worship.

Each offer was a trap, a distraction from His mission, yet Jesus, wielding the sword of Scripture, cut through the dragon's lies and defeated Satan's purposes. In his book *The Cost of Discipleship*, Dietrich Bonhoeffer lays bare the battle with temptation. Bonhoeffer warns that the cost of following Christ is high because it demands total allegiance, a resistance to the easy, sinful paths that tempt us, even when they promise the world.

Yet, beyond the dragon of temptation lie two priceless treasures. The treasure of purity, sparkling like a diamond with the clarity of a conscience untainted by sin, and the treasure of spiritual integrity, a fortress akin to a life lived in alignment with God's will. These treasures are truly the essence of a life that reflects the light of Christ. Imagine the strength that comes from these. No longer swayed by every passing allure, you stand firm, anchored in purity and integrity. By staying vigilant (1 Peter 5:8), and keeping your eyes fixed on Jesus, the author and perfecter of your faith (Hebrews 12:2), you can slay temptation. By immersing yourself in God's word and using it as a shield against the dragon's fiery darts (Ephesians 6:16), you can dilute their power. By surrounding yourself with a community of believers who encourage and hold you accountable you can repel sin's grip. Each act of resistance and each moment of integrity is a blow to the dragon's seductive influence. And just like the previous four dragons, the *dragon of temptation* is a cunning foe, but not an unconquerable one. With each act of purity, each steadfast refusal of sin, you weaken its grip and draw closer to the treasures that God has prepared for you. Don't be swayed by fleeting pleasures, but rather find true fulfillment in purity and integrity.

Dragons and Treasures 6
(Unforgiveness)

Be kind and compassionate to one another, forgiving each other,
just as in Christ God forgave you.
Ephesians 4:32

Deep in the cavern of our soul there lies a dragon that thrives on bitterness. It festers quietly, spreading its poison, turning sweet memories into bitter ones. This is the *dragon of unforgiveness.* Unforgiveness is a silent killer, creeping into our lives through unresolved hurts and unspoken grievances. It wraps around our hearts, squeezing out compassion and replacing it with resentment. Ephesians 4:32 pleads with us, "Be kind and compassionate to one another, forgiving each other, just as in Christ God forgave you." But unforgiveness reminds us of every slight, wound, and reason to hold on to our pain. I haven't struggled much with unforgiveness, thank God, but I've seen how destructive it can be.

I knew a pastor once who was a bright man, though he relied more on his intellect than on the guidance of the Holy Spirit. Every week, he wrote his Sunday sermon on scraps of paper and then gave them to me to type up and email to the newspaper for publication. One evening, after finishing most of the meal his wife had made, he left a piece of meat on his plate, intending to eat it later. Unaware of this, his wife ate the leftover meat while clearing the dishes, a tiny misunderstanding that erupted into verbal abuse and physical confrontation. He wouldn't forgive her. Things spiraled from there for the pastor. Plagued by patterns of unforgiveness, he fell into sexual immorality with women in the neighborhood and was eventually publicly disgraced and forced to leave town. Unforgiveness gave the enemy a foothold in his life, and the devil, true to form, exploited it. If we allow unforgiveness to take root, it will only open the door for greater destruction.

Consider the parable of the unforgiving servant. A king forgave his servant a massive debt, an amount so large it could never be repaid, but this servant turned around and demanded repayment from a fellow servant who owed him a pittance. When the king heard of this, he was furious and handed the unforgiving servant over to the tormentors. Jesus' message is clear: forgiveness received must be forgiveness extended. In my simple way, I see the word *forgive* and split it into two parts: *for* and *give*. Something is meant to be given, not held tightly in our unyielding grasp.

Lewis B. Smedes, in his profound book, *Forgive and Forget*, delves into the power and necessity of forgiveness. Smedes describes forgiveness as setting a prisoner free, only to discover that the prisoner was you. He highlights that forgiveness is not about condoning wrongs or forgetting pain, but about releasing ourselves from the chains of resentment.

Unforgiveness is the voice that says, "They don't deserve your forgiveness. Hold on to your anger. Protect yourself." Yet, beyond the dragon of unforgiveness lies a treasure that is worth the battle—the treasure of peace, which is a balm for our souls, soothing the wounds that bitterness has left behind. Peace ensures that we no longer have to carry the heavy burden of past wrongs. We can walk lightly, unburdened by the chains of resentment, and the storms of anger and bitterness can no longer rage. Relationships are restored, and trust and love can grow once more. By choosing to forgive, even when it feels impossible, we are giving ourselves a gift as much as we are giving it to others. We are imitating Christ, who forgave us even as we nailed Him to the cross.

Like the previous five dragons, the *dragon of unforgiveness* is a formidable foe, but not an invincible one. Each act of forgiveness, each release of resentment, weakens its hold and moves you closer to the treasures God has for you. You don't have to be a prisoner of your own making; you can find the peace and restored relationships that come from forgiving as you have been forgiven. The treasure that lies beyond this dragon is a trove of healing that cleanses your soul and transforms your heart and your life.

Downfall

All at once he followed her, like an ox going to the slaughter.
Proverbs 7:22

When I was a young believer, I witnessed a plot of the enemy unfold against the leader of a church first-hand. This church was fairly large, being of about 1200 members, and was the very first church I attended regularly. The pastor was a very charismatic and handsome man. He was always surrounded by crowds on Sunday mornings before the service began, but when he spotted me he would cut through them and rush toward me with a very intense look on his face. When he reached me, he would grab my hands with his and pierce me with his eyes. "I want you to know I love you," he would say. "I really do. And God loves you too."

This had a profound effect on me. I was fresh from the world—some of the darkness of it was still clinging to me—but my insecurities about God's love melted away under this man's ministry. When he gave the call for baptisms one week, I felt a stronger pull than any I've experienced before or since. His anointing was that strong. So, I was heartbroken to witness the following:

One Sunday morning my view of the pastor as he was giving his message was blocked by two young women who I'd never seen before. They sat directly in front of me and spent the entire service whispering and pointing at the pastor while he spoke. I was a new believer, but I could sense that something was wrong. The two women had brought something into the service with them that had no reverence for God. This pointing and whispering continued for about six weeks, and then one Sunday morning the pastor and the two women were nowhere to be seen. After a short message, an elder broke the news that the pastor had left the church and his family (he was married and had two children) to be with the prettier and more animated of the two whispering women. And that was that. My first pastor—my first spiritual covering—was gone.

A couple years later, I met a very Godly and prophetic woman who took me under her wings and taught me everything she knew about intercessory prayer. This led to my habit of making prayer lists and the fallen pastor's name ended up near the top of one of them. Lo and behold, I walked out of a business one day and looked over to see the ex-pastor walking nearly parallel to me out of another business. I called out his name, but the man who used to run to greet me made a dash for his car when he saw who I was. I was determined, though. I caught up with him just as he shut his car door and banged enthusiastically on his window until he rolled it down. "Do you remember me?" I said. "I certainly do," he said, and proceeded to tell me how he was still serving God with his new life insurance business. The radiance was gone, however, as was his spark of confidence. When he pulled away I felt sad and stunned by the devil's crafty and demoralizing handiwork.

This occurred about 30 years ago, and I'm reminded of a scripture as I write this: *Strike the shepherd and the sheep will scatter.* (Zechariah 13:7) It describes the circumstance exactly. It took that pastor's church many years to shake off the residues of scandal and injured faith and rebuild its foundations all over again. A lot of people were hurt. But even back then, even with my naive faith, I could see like a laser beam through the smoke how the enemy was working. Did those women know they had been sent in by the devil?

What was their level of culpability? I don't know, but this is what God has told me: "There was a plan from the enemy, and prayer could have overturned it, but nobody was praying for that pastor and his family in a concentrated, effectual way."

Intercessory prayer is this: Praying to God on behalf of others (standing in the gap for them) and speaking with authority against the enemy's efforts to overthrow them.

So, be on guard. Pray and then pray some more for your pastors, leaders, family, and friends. And then pray some more even after that. It works. It's powerful. It can, and will, overturn and prevent disastrous calamities just like the one I've described here.

Mastering The Monster

Then the Lord said to Cain, 'Why are you angry? Why is your face downcast?
Genesis 4:6

I didn't struggle with anger for long, but it was an issue I had to confront at some point. Growing up as the last child in my family, I observed and learned from the mistakes of my older siblings, which helped me to avoid many pitfalls. However, anger ran in my family. It wasn't something we talked about openly, but I could see how it affected us in different ways. The enemy was always ready to exploit our weaknesses. One particular incident stands out to me. I was serving as a volunteer member in a youth ministry back in Nigeria, a role that involved arriving early to help set up the auditorium and prepare for the service.

One day, during the usual pre-service routine, I had a disagreement with a fellow team member, a young lady who was kind and patient as a rule. For some reason, the disagreement escalated, and before I knew it, I was yelling at her at the top of my lungs. If you had seen me, you would have laughed. I was seventeen years old, but I looked like a scrawny twelve-year-old kid. My size often made me feel like people didn't take me seriously, and in that moment, I let insecurity fuel my rage. I shouted at her, using hurtful words that shocked everyone, including myself! My reaction was completely out of proportion to the situation.

Immediately after my outburst, I realized how foolish I'd been and walked away in shame. Later, I returned to apologize, and she forgave me easily. That moment is etched in my memory. I realized the importance of mastering my emotions so they wouldn't control me, and with God's help, I've since learned to respond to conflict with patience and self-control. Untamed anger is a dark force, a monster, lurking in the shadows of our minds, waiting for a moment of weakness to pounce.

Stephen R. Covey, in his insightful work, *The 8th Habit*, captures this phenomenon with chilling clarity: "Between stimulus and response, there's a space. In that space lies our power to choose our response. In that response lies our growth and freedom." Covey's quote conveys a crucial truth. The space between what provokes us and how we react is our sanctuary, a place where we can wrestle with our instincts and emerge victorious. This space is our arena for growth and the gateway to our liberation.

Consider the biblical story of Cain and Abel. It's a story as old as time, yet it remains starkly relevant. Cain, enraged by God's rejection of his offering, allowed his anger to cause him to commit the first murder recorded in the Bible. However, between the sting of rejection and the act of fratricide, there was a moment—a space—where Cain had the opportunity to choose a different path.

God Himself warned Cain: "If you do what is right, will you not be accepted? But if you do not do what is right, sin is crouching at your door; it desires to have you, but you must master it." (Genesis 4:6, 7) Cain could have chosen to reflect, to understand his anger, and to respond differently, but he didn't. His story serves as a grim reminder of the destruction untamed anger can wreak. Anger doesn't just harm those directly involved; its tendrils reach out, leaving lasting damage to bystanders and relationships.

Paul's advice in Ephesians is a beacon in such times: "In your anger do not sin: Do not let the sun go down while you are still angry, and do not give the devil a foothold." (Ephesians 4:26, 27) This admonition to resolve anger quickly and not let it fester is a crucial strategy for preventing sin and maintaining our integrity.

The power of your response to anger lies in your ability to pause, reflect, and choose wisely. This ability transforms you, helps you grow, and ultimately sets you free from the chains of your base impulses. It is in this deliberate response that you will find your path to true freedom and the strength to master this debilitating monster.

God's Timing and Trusting His Process

Once the battle begins, patience and trust in God's timing are vital. Believers must persevere through delays and trials by trusting God's process.

And Then I Met Eric

Do not be anxious about anything, but in every situation, by prayer and petition, with thanksgiving, present your requests to God. And the peace of God, which transcends all understanding, will guard your hearts and your minds in Christ Jesus.
Philippians 4:6, 7

In life, I've come to realize that what we often dismiss as mere coincidences are, in truth, the meticulous workings of divine providence. Nothing surprises God; nothing is left to chance or mistake. The same Creator who set the planets in their precise orbits, who maintains the delicate balance of the universe, is the God who orchestrates the events of our lives with perfect precision. He's a marvelous God, who works all things together for good (Romans 8:28). One of the most profound illustrations of this truth in my life unfolded during a journey that forever changed my perspective.

It was the 10th of March, 2012. Financial constraints had forced me to withdraw from my school in Florida. My destination? A Bible school in Tulsa, Oklahoma. After securing my bus ticket, I found myself at the Greyhound station in Pensacola, filled with a mixture of uncertainty and hope. The journey began smoothly, but when we reached Shreveport, Louisiana, things started to unravel. Buses were delayed, and I missed several connections, supposedly due to a time change.

Frustration crept in, but little did I know these delays were part of a grander plan. After missing two more buses, I finally boarded one bound for Dallas, Texas. During the prolonged wait at the station, I found solace in reading my Bible and praying. Initially, my prayers were requests for swifter progress, born out of impatience, but as the hours passed, my prayers evolved. I began to ask God to reveal His purpose in these delays. Soon, a sense of peace enveloped me, a weight lifted off my shoulders, and I realized this was the peace that comes from trusting God completely (Philippians 4:6-7).

When my bus arrived in Dallas, it was late due to a storm, causing me to miss yet another connection. But this time, I felt no frustration, only peace and gratitude. I approached the customer service desk, only to be told that the next bus to Tulsa wouldn't arrive until the following day. My travel plans were in disarray, but my heart was calm. I prayed once more, asking God to reveal the purpose of these mishaps before I left Dallas.

And then I met Eric.

Eric was a fellow traveler, and as we waited, we struck up a conversation. What began as casual small talk soon delved into deeper topics, and I felt a nudge to share my faith with him. To my astonishment, Eric was open and eager to hear more. That day, in the midst of a bustling bus station, Eric decided to give his life to Jesus. He was the first person I led to Christ. We exchanged contact information and kept in touch for several years. The last I heard, he had found a good church and was growing in his faith.

Reflecting on that journey, I see how every delay, every missed connection, was a divine appointment leading to Eric's salvation. What seemed like chaos was actually a beautifully orchestrated plan. Trusting in God's timing and purpose, I learned that our paths, no matter how uncertain they seem, are guided by His unfailing hand. Trust Him, He knows what He's doing. Only be humble enough to seek Him for wisdom and discernment in those moments when you don't understand why things aren't going the way you think they should.

In Due Time

To everything, there is a season and a time for every matter under heaven.
Ecclesiastes 3:1

I've desired to be married since the age of 16. I wasn't even a high school graduate yet, but I thought I had cracked the code of being a great partner, perhaps even an enviable dad. I was friendly and approachable, the kid in high school that everyone liked but the girls weren't interested in dating. There's more to that story, but I'll save it for another article. Eventually, I got married. I was 31. A few years later, when I was 33, my first child was born. Now I understand that marriage is not child's play. It takes work and maturity, and God, in His infinite wisdom, knew when I would be ready for that particular blessing and challenged me to be patient until His appointed time arrived.

Do you find yourself yearning for material possessions like riches, a car, a house, or a relationship with that special someone dear to your heart? If these things are truly what you desire, rest assured that God will grant them to you. It's possible, however, that they are not what you need at this present moment. Perhaps, instead of material wealth, what you truly need is an increase in faith, something spiritual rather than tangible. You may need patience more than a relationship, and contentment rather than a car. It might even be that you need to learn the grace of giving instead of acquiring another house.

We live in a world where immediate gratification is prized and where waiting is seen as a weakness, but God's timeline is not ours. His ways are higher, His thoughts deeper, and His understanding perfect. As Isaiah 55:8, 9 says, "For my thoughts are not your thoughts, neither are your ways my ways," declares the Lord. "As the heavens are higher than the earth, so are my ways higher than your ways and my thoughts than your thoughts."

When you find yourself waiting, understand that God may be working on something within you, something far more valuable than the object of your desire. Maybe He's building your character, deepening your faith, or teaching you patience. Remember, delay is not denial. It's a strategic pause that serves a higher purpose. Jesus himself said in Matthew 6:8, "Your Father knows what you need before you ask Him." Trust that He knows your needs better than you do.

Ecclesiastes 3:1 reminds us, "To everything, there is a season and a time for every matter under heaven." Your season of waiting is not wasted time. It's God's way of aligning your heart with His perfect will. Sometimes, He withholds what we want to give us what we need, and that often means spiritual riches over material wealth, patience over immediate gratification, and contentment over constant striving.

God is never late and seldom early, but He is always precisely on time. This divine punctuality ensures that we receive what we need exactly when we need it. His timing helps us grow in our faith and align more closely with His will. The waiting room of life is where we learn to trust in God's provision and timing, where our faith is forged and our character refined.

The Crucible of Egypt

You intended to harm me, but God intended it for good to accomplish what is now being done, the saving of many lives.
Genesis 50:20

What's your own Egypt? Your *Egypt* might be a situation or place where you find yourself unexpectedly or unwillingly. It could be a difficult job, a challenging relationship, or a season of life that feels like a detour. Egypt, in its symbolic essence, is a crucible of trial and growth—a preparation ground where you can be refined, developed, and matured. Several biblical figures walked through Egypt's scorching sands, only to emerge stronger and more prepared for their divine missions.

Consider Abraham, who journeyed to Egypt during a famine (Genesis 12:10). He went willingly, but the land of the Pharaohs was still a testing ground for his faith. Then there's Joseph, thrust into Egypt against his will, and sold into slavery by his own brothers. Yet, Egypt became the forge that tempered his spirit and prepared him for greatness. Through trials and tribulations, he grew in wisdom, leadership, and faith. Ultimately, he rose to power, saving not just Egypt but also his family from famine. Genesis 50:20 captures the essence of his journey: "You intended to harm me, but God intended it for good to accomplish what is now being done, the saving of many lives." Even Jesus spent time in Egypt. As a child, He was taken there by Mary and Joseph to escape King Herod's massacre. This sojourn in Egypt was crucial for His protection and preparation until it was safe to return and fulfill His ministry.

Understand that Egypt is not merely a place of hardship but is a divine setup— a launchpad into your next season. The devil might lead us into places of disappointment through our own mistakes or circumstances beyond our control, but God can transform these places into appointments for growth and preparation. When we acknowledge our errors and repent, God uses these challenging times as our Egypt— a place where we are equipped, developed, and matured into who He has called us to be.

Reflect on your life and identify the *Egypts* you have experienced or are currently enduring. These are the places or situations where you feel challenged or out of place. These experiences are not wasted. Embrace them as opportunities for growth and preparation. In your Egypt, seek God's guidance and strength. Trust that He is with you and that He is using this time to prepare you for what lies ahead. Look at disappointments as divine appointments. Allow God to transform your perspective and use these times to shape you into the person He wants you to be. Let your Egypt be the forge that hones you, the fire that refines you, and the crucible that prepares you for the divine purpose ahead. Just as Joseph and Jesus emerged from Egypt to fulfill their destinies, so too will you rise, ready for the mission God has set before you.

The Stump

As a terebinth tree or an oak tree when it is cut down,
so the Holy Seed shall be its stump.
Isaiah 6:13

Seeds are incredible things. They are arguably God's greatest creation as their durable coatings allow them to survive fire, water, and time without any ill effect. In 2005, a Jewish doctor named Sarah Sallon, stunned the world when she successfully germinated a 2000-year-old date seed. When the plant grew, it was found to not be stunted or misshapen in any way. The seed produced what it was intended to produce.

What has God spoken to you? His personal declarations to you are word seeds, and once they are planted, the seasons must then be allowed to pass. Time is really the ultimate test of all things, isn't it? Fiery trials may test our works and throw raging whirlwinds of doubt at us, but time is really the bigger challenge. Who likes to wait, after all? A wonderfully astute and faith-filled minister friend once told me, "Greg, people get it wrong. They think of great faith in terms of volume, like a cup being filled with water, but faith is linear and is measured out along a timeline. How long will a person keep believing something God has told them before they stumble into doubt and walk away from it?"

We see this idea demonstrated all throughout the Bible. Jesus rebuked His disciples for worrying about food after watching Him turn a few loaves of bread into enough food to feed thousands. Their faith ran out after only a few hours. Conversely, Abraham is called a hero of the faith because he waited for 27 years for a promise to be fulfilled, and at a point when his body was nearly dead from old age. This is God's goal, to develop us to a level where He can speak a thing and then 20 years pass without us hearing from Him again, yet we still believe.

There are seeds, and then there are stumps. A stump is the leftover of a cut-down promise. Something happened. Calamity struck. It's the kind of thing that makes a believer cry out, "Why have you forsaken me, Lord? Where is your goodness?" But destruction is the most holy of all situations when it occurs on the soil of promise, for the prospect of a miracle greater than the seed itself is on the horizon. God hasn't forgotten what He said. He hasn't been taken by surprise. A seed on its own is a miraculous thing, but the glory of a seed resurrected is ten-thousand times as exciting. The testimony about it reaches the ears of multitudes, and God is glorified in ways that the first and original miracle wasn't able to accomplish.

I want you to know this: your child Isaac is about to be unbound, and your dead Lazarus is about to be called forth from his tomb. If you and your promise have been chosen for suffering, rejoice, because God wants to demonstrate something to the enemy. He is going to demonstrate that promises survive death itself. Here is what God says to you, the sufferer: "There is hope for a tree if it is cut down. At the first scent of water, it will bud again like a young plant." (Job 14:9) When is the water coming? Only God knows, but it surely will. Wait as faithfully for the resurrection as you did for the seed. This is your final test because, "God is not a man that He should lie." (Numbers 23:18) He will perform what He said He will perform and make a hero of the faith out of you in the process.

Yesterday's Provision in Tomorrow's Home

(The Most Difficult Transition)

And the manna continued until the day after they had eaten from the produce of the land.
Joshua 5:12

If you are reaching for God's best for you, at some point you will find yourself straddling both the past and the future at the same time. The scenery has changed but your job hasn't. You're still doing what you've done forever and but without any grace for it. You feel like you're wrapped in lead chains. Israel's conquest of the promised land began this way as well. They walked out of the *desert of toil* (where they had scraped manna from the hard desert floor for forty long years), following God's whirlwind, only to find themselves toiling once more within sight of Jericho's palm trees, orange groves, and vineyards. They were in paradise, but when they stepped out of their tents that first morning, there was the manna again, covering the grassy Canaan riverbank like a thin layer of frost. Would they ever catch a break? Yes. They couldn't see it, but they were only a week away from permanent, irreversible change.

God's first command came immediately: keep the Passover (which lasted seven days—not so long) and circumcise their men. This can be seen as a complete and resolute dedication to doing things God's way only. Consecration. During this time the manna continued to fall. Finally, on the eighth day, the manna fell for a final time. It would never be seen on earth again. Similarly, the day will come for you when the manner in which you were formerly provided for is no longer your lot.

The only way is to go forward and eat from the produce of the land.

There's a great scripture in the book of Genesis that talks about Isaac's journey into prosperity: "The man began to prosper and continued prospering until he became very prosperous." (Genesis 26:13) His wealth came in stages. Not everything has to do with money, but a good many things do. If you own cows, they need to be fed. If your business employs people, they need accommodations, equipment, and electricity. God wants to bless you so profoundly that you can be a blessing to others, but it all starts on the banks of the Jordan River in that strange twilight encampment where the past isn't yours anymore, but the future isn't yet either. It is one of the holiest places you'll ever visit in your Christian walk.

It was there on the banks of the Jordan River, with the smell of mud and fish in his nose, that Joshua encountered the Commander of the Armies of the Lord who told him, "Take the sandals off your feet, for the place you are standing on is Holy Ground." (Joshua 5:15) It is the entrance to destiny. It is the starting line of the race the Apostle Paul is referring to when he says to "press toward the goal for the prize of the high calling." (Philippians 3:14) God would like to encourage you now. Although you have never passed this way before, the territory ahead is a good land, one worth fighting for. Others are depending on you. And, although you can't see it, you may be only a short time away from permanent, irreversible change.

Press on. Press in. Understand that transitions are temporary but necessary. The Commander of the Armies of the Lord calls every one of them Holy Ground.

The Four Kingdoms

The first living creature was like a lion, the second like a calf, the third like a man, and the fourth like an eagle.
Revelation 4:6, 7

The sea of crystal mentioned in Revelation 4:6 extends outwards from the base of God's throne like a stage and is populated by a variety of characters. God and Jesus, along with twenty-four elders, sit at the center of everything while four strange creatures stand at posts directly in front of them. The first creature resembles a lion, the second a calf or an ox, the third a man, and the fourth an eagle. They each have six wings and are covered with many eyes and praise God continually. These are the ambassadors of the four kingdoms God loves the most in all of His creation: the *Kingdom of Men*, the *Kingdom of Domesticated Animals*, the *Kingdom of Wild Animals*, and the *Kingdom of Birds*. These are His favorites, and the many eyes of these creatures are constantly scanning the condition of their realms to give a report, after which God answers them and meets every individual creature need according to the bounty of His supply. "Look at the birds, who neither sow nor reap, yet your Heavenly Father feeds them," we are told in Matthew 6:26. And Psalm 104:21 informs us that, "The young lions roar after their prey and seek their meal from God," and God is faithful to provide for them. He loves His creation that intensely.

But how do we know these strange winged and multi-eyed creatures aren't simply symbols of spiritual things? We know because when they begin to praise God, the elders respond instantly by falling to their knees to thank God for the physical world that we can see, feel, touch, taste, and smell, and everything that inhabits it. "You are worthy!" they cry, "for You created all things and by Your will they exist and were created." (Revelation 4:11) Everything spiritual and eternal pauses as God is extolled for this present and very natural creation that you and I know so well.

This is astonishing because we tend to think of birds and animals as temporary, passing creatures—brief flickers of life unworthy of eternal representation. But look, their ambassadors have places directly in front of God's throne! They may be a level below human beings in terms of the war between good and evil—they weren't created in God's image—but they are still unique individuals with distinct personalities and God loves them. Jesus died for creation too. In fact, we are told in Romans 8 that all of creation is groaning in anticipation of redemption from the grip of death. It's a fantastic thing to think about. Imagine what the wild outlands of Heaven must look like.

When we ponder the dense thickets of a jungle or the depths of an ocean, and all that they hold, we are catching only a glimpse of God's creative capabilities. He has so much more in store for us, and for His creatures. As 1 Corinthians 2:9 reminds us: "Eye has not seen nor ear heard, nor have entered into the heart of man the things which God has prepared for those who love Him."

Overcoming Strongholds and Principalities

Following trust in God's timing, it becomes necessary to face and dismantle strongholds and spiritual forces that hinder growth. This naturally progresses from understanding crisis and delay.

Euroclydon

But not long after, a tempestuous head wind arose, called Euroclydon.
Acts 27:14

In Acts 27, the Apostle Paul—prisoner and survivor—finds himself on a ship bound for Rome, a city that holds his fate through the grip of Caesar's hand. The journey is supposed to be straightforward, but nature has other plans. The winds are calm at first, lulling the crew into a dangerous sense of security. But Paul, with a foresight that comes only from divine discernment, warns them. "Men, I perceive that this voyage will end with disaster and much loss, not only of the cargo and ship but also our lives." (Acts 27:10) The captain and crew dismiss his words, though. After all, what does a prisoner know about the sea's temperament? Then comes the storm, and it has a name: *Euroclydon.*

Euroclydon is a tempest, a howling beast born in the autumn skies of the Mediterranean. Verse 14 captures the moment it strikes: "Not long after, a tempestuous head wind called Euroclydon arose," and for captain and convict alike, the relentless, unforgiving storm would become a test of endurance.

For today's Christian, Euroclydon is a symbol, a metaphor for the tempests that rise when we chart our course by our own understanding, ignoring the voice of God and the clear signs he gives us. It's a mistake we make time and again. We trust our own judgment, confident in our expertise, and then find ourselves in the middle of a storm we never saw coming. Suddenly, our ship is tossed, battered, and beaten by waves that seem to rise up from the abyss.

Here's the truth: when we ignore God's warnings, we end up in situations where our own strength, wisdom, and self-efforts mean nothing. The storm overwhelms us. Hope dims and despair creeps in.

Sometimes the journey is God-ordained, but sometimes the storm could have been avoided if only we had listened. We lean on what we know, on what we see, on winds that seem favorable—until they turn on us.

In Acts 27, the sailors fought the storm with everything they had, but their battle was lost before it began. They weren't just fighting Euroclydon; they were fighting the consequences of their own disobedience. Yet, in the eye of the storm, there is Paul—calm, resolute, anchored by a faith that doesn't bend to the wind. He stands, not as a man broken by the tempest, but as one who hears from God. "For there stood by me this night an angel of the God to whom I belong and whom I serve, saying, 'Do not be afraid, Paul; you must be brought before Caesar; and indeed, God has granted you all those who sail with you.'" (Acts 27:23, 24). Paul's faith became the lifeline for everyone aboard that ship. He trusted, not in the ship or the skill of the sailors, but in the promise of God. That trust saved not only him but also everyone else on board.

This is where we are called to reflect, to look at the storms in our own lives. Are we caught in a Euroclydon of our own making? Have we ignored the still, small voice of God, only to find ourselves in a tempest that could have been avoided? The way out is clear: return to God's path. Trust His guidance. Obey His instructions. Only then can we make it through the storm and arrive at the destination He has prepared for us.

The story of Euroclydon is a mirror, illustrating the consequences of disobedience and the power of trust in God's sovereignty. Even in the midst of a storm, God's voice cuts through the howl of the wind and will guide us back to safety. Following God's instructions isn't just a good idea—it's a lifesaver. It's the difference between shipwreck and salvation. When we trust Him, even the fiercest Euroclydon becomes a backdrop for His power and grace, a stage on which His glory is revealed.

Giants In Detail 1
(Sihon)

For Heshbon was the city of Sihon king of the Amorites.
Numbers 21:26

Almost right from the beginning there have been giants on the earth, both physical and spiritual, and sooner or later we're going to be led by God to encounters with them. But God is a God of processes and when He sets an adversary before us, there is purpose in it beyond merely strengthening us or testing our endurance. There is insight to be gained. We come to better understand the various temptations the devil uses to try to undermine the vitality of our walk with God.

When King David was young, he defeated a lion and a bear before stepping onto the battlefield to face Goliath. These weren't random events. The lion represented willfulness, the bear represented fear, and Goliath represented doubt, and there was design in the order in which David was confronted by them. God works the same way with us.

To step into the best life God has for us, we must defeat a series of giants in stages, each of whom represents a spiritual test. The first of these is Sihon, the Amorite king described in the 21st chapter of the book of Numbers. His name means "tempestuous," which refers to the instability and double mindedness of our fleshly natures. He was the first giant the Israelites faced on their trek through the wilderness.

The battle with Sihon—our own stubbornness—is a crucial one for many reasons. For one, it is the first of the "possession battles," as there is territory to be had for successfully conquering Sihon. In the book of Numbers, God gave Sihon's lands and its two rivers, the Arnon ("a glad stream") and the Jabbok ("a pouring forth") to three of the tribes of Israel for successfully defeating him. (Numbers 21:24, 25)

Victory over Sihon also signals to the enemy that God is beginning to maneuver a believer into His highest purpose for them. In the book of Joshua, the news of Sihon's defeat reached the city of Jericho where the people's hearts melted, leaving "no spirit left in any man." (Joshua 2:11)

Sihon won't fall easily, though. Humans are stubborn, aren't we? Up to this point, we have done whatever we pleased, and in whatever manner we chose, but we can't remain a tempest and go forward with God. James 1:7, 8 tells us that he who is "blown and tossed by the wind should not expect to receive anything from the Lord."

Here is how my own battle with Sihon transpired: A friend of mine named Gerry became my pastor almost overnight, causing me to have to submit to him in ways that challenged my pride and independence. Previously, we were equal in every way, typical friends living typical lives, but then God spoke to me clearly one day, "I want you to serve this man and help him build the church he is starting." Everything changed instantly. Whether I agreed with him or not, I was to serve Gerry faithfully and use all the gifts and talents at my disposal to help advance his efforts. I couldn't call him "Gerry" anymore either. I had to call him "Pastor Gerry," and always honor the office that he stood in.

This switch in the dynamics of our relationship was difficult. So was becoming part of a team. Everything in me wanted to bolt and run, but deep down I knew that if I did, I would be running from my own future. Over and over again, God reminded me, "If you continue to obey me and serve the man I raised up over you faithfully, I will bring you into your own promised land one day." It wasn't a stripping away of dignity so much—God wants us to be confident—but my island mentality had to go. If I wanted to be a leader myself, I needed to learn how to follow first. In the end, I came through a transformed man. God could say "Go here," and I wouldn't hesitate.

Sihon lay dead. And what was my reward? Joy. Those two rivers— the Arnon and the Jabbok. And promotions as well. I began to move into my own place of prominence and purpose, while a future I could never have imagined began to rise up around me. I did things and went places I never dreamed were possible. Now, I was ready to face Og of Bashan, the next giant.

Giants In Detail 2
(Og)

So Og, King of Bashan, went out against them, he and all his people.
Numbers 21:33

Og is the second giant that we will face when we are marching towards God's highest and best life for us. Og means *round* or *full*. Similar to Sihon, the first giant, Og has to do with the flesh and the manner in which its appetites affect and impede our faithful service to God. The real life Og was enormous. His bed was thirteen feet long so overcoming him will take moving from being appetite-led to Spirit-led, a challenging task after living a lifetime doing whatever we want.

In the simplest example I can think of, here is the challenge of the flesh: A man has two cups of coffee every morning at 7 a.m. for years—day in and day out—until he is convinced that he can't function normally without them. Then, when God comes at 7 a.m. one day and says "pray," the man will refuse. He hasn't had his coffee yet. How then would he follow instructions in the heat of a battle? Because that's what this is all about—doing what God says to do when we feel like doing something else.

A mentor shared the same idea with me when I was still a young believer. He told me, "If you can't say no to the extra cookie, you may not be able to say no to the extra-marital affair." Routines are Og's heartbeat. I heard this story told of a well-known man of God: Jesus appeared to him personally one night in his hotel room and said, "I could have done so much more with you if it wasn't for that habit of yours." He wouldn't share what the habit was, but admitted "It was akin to having a piece of pie at the very same time every night. It wasn't sinful, but it was something I wouldn't let go of."

My own victory over Og came when I got the revelation that living a "fasted lifestyle" does a better job at managing the flesh than traditional fasting. To me, "a fasted lifestyle," means saying no to one's flesh in mostly small areas on a daily basis. It might mean skipping lunch one day, saying no TV the next, then cutting out snacks on the third. Deliberate choices that let the flesh know that the spiritual "inner man" is in charge, not the body. Over a span of time, these types of flesh denials create an inner strength and fine tune our spiritual eyes and ears to the Spirit of God. Hesitancy is reduced and instant obedience becomes as natural as breathing. However you do it, the goal is the same: to become someone that God can rely on.

Ultimately, after a few years of retraining my flesh, I got to the point where abiding in God's presence was enough. Where I had been rigid before, I was pliable, and although my flesh still clamored for rewards—food, drink, and entertainment—its voice had been reduced from a shout to a whisper. I was determined to keep it that way. I encourage you to see this battle through, no matter how difficult. After Og, the promised land comes into view. The next giant, the King of Jericho, is waiting, and he is formidable. If we are stiff with habits when God says, "March silently around the city for seven days," sluggishness could lead to missing our time.

Giants In Detail 3
(The King of Jericho)

See, I have given into your hand Jericho, and the king thereof.
Joshua 6:1-5

The next battle in our march towards living the best life God has for us involves the King of Jericho, a title that can be interpreted as *the fragrance of the moon.* From times past, the moon has always represented the mind, making this battle—a command from God to trust Him in spite of all that we see, feel or understand—perhaps the most challenging of them all. And whereas Satan had little to do with our struggles against Sihon and Og, he has everything to do with this one. The idea is simple: God will bring a believer to the first experience in his life where success or failure depends implicitly on following a singular logic-defying instruction. It won't make sense, tempting us to act rashly and take the matter into our own hands.

For the Israelites, the instruction was, "You shall march around the city one time for six days, then seven times on the seventh. Then, when the trumpet sounds, shout!" (Joshua 6:2-5.) So, the Israelites marched as they were directed, but the first six days ended the same way, with Jericho's anxious citizens finding themselves secure once again behind their city's thick walls. Day after day, nothing changed. Finally, the appointed hour came and when the trumpet sounded and the shout was given, the city's walls didn't just collapse—they fell flat. The key was following God's instructions to the letter.

In my own battle with the King of Jericho the instruction was, "Stand still and see the salvation of the Lord." (Exodus 14:13) Very much like the situation with the Israelites, I had been on a long journey with God—twenty years of moving toward a specific destination—

when I ran into an immovable wall in the form of a high-ranking official in church. "I don't want you on the worship team anymore," she told me. "I have someone else in mind for that position." I knew I was in God's will, but God told me not to argue about the situation or try to defend myself. I was to stay silent and trust. So, I went home and did absolutely nothing until the worship team's main vocalist called me a short time later. "I heard what happened," she said, "but the pastor has authorized me to make decisions concerning the worship team, and I want to keep you on it. See you Sunday at practice." And that was that.

Everything relating to the next twenty years of my life—and I can't understate this—hinged upon that single event and my decision to trust God to work things out. And the official who tried to replace me? The next time I saw her she was all smiles and gratitude, and we never had another issue. It had all been a test.

So, hold fast. Be prepared to walk to the edge of a cliff if necessary. Do whatever God asks of you without questioning it, no matter how illogical the instruction seems. If you don't learn to trust God, Jericho is as far as you will get. And there is so much more beyond those towering walls. A vista awaits, the wide expanse of the promised land and the life you were created to live. Something else awaits as well, the King of the city of Ai, who will test your allegiance to God to the core. Hold fast. The journey is about to get exciting.

Giants In Detail 4
(The King of Ai)

You shall do to Ai and its king as you did to Jericho,
except you may keep the plunder for yourselves.
Joshua 8:2

After a Christian has defeated the King of Jericho, God leads him into the interior of the promised land. There, the King of Ai awaits him with jeers, flashing swords, and a demonic scowl. Ai means *ruins*, and this is a believer's first battle with the *Greater Temptations*. Up to this point, the struggle has always been directly connected to the flesh and obedience.

"The basics," a pastor friend of mine once called them. Cussing, drinking, fornication, overindulgence and impulsiveness. But each of us holds the potential to sin in ways we could never have imagined. Spiritual sins. Subtle wickedness that can lead to catastrophic errors. When King David cried out, "See if there be any wicked way in me," (Psalm 139:23, 24), this is what he was referring to. He recognized that although he was a Godly man, his heart had the potential to lean the wrong way.

You and I have the same potential. We think we know ourselves, but the spiritual test that the King of Ai represents will press us like a vice. Can the devil ruin us? He wants to see, and this is how it will occur: God will say no to something that we highly desire and both he and the devil will watch to see how we respond. "That's mine," God will declare. "Don't even go near it. I've reserved it for myself." In Joshua's day, it was plunder from Jericho. The Israelites were told not to keep anything for themselves. For you and I, the item that is off-limits could be a romantic relationship, a business venture, or a ministry position. It will seem *so* right—compelling beyond measure—but it is deadly. God will not budge or change His mind about the matter for all eternity. It is either obedience or face the consequences, which can be severe.

To illustrate this, in Joshua 7, the Israelites lost their first battle with the King of Ai because a man name Achan kept some of Jericho's treasures for himself. Thirty-six Israelites died as a result, as did Achan and his entire family. They were the first casualties of the promised land. I myself failed to defeat the King of Ai on my first pass. I wouldn't walk away from a wrong romantic relationship and the consequences of my disobedience left me with permanent scars. Just as with the Israelites, I did get to take the test again (and I passed it), but the original losses were never recovered. Jesus appeared to me for the first and only time not long after that, and although He acknowledged my error, His presence brought with it a sense of love, grace and encouragement for the future.

So, what *is* the reward for walking away from a denied thing? Everything beyond it. The entire length and breadth of the promised land, with all of its bright walled cities and the treasures contained therein. Nothing is held back. After Joshua and the Israelites repented of Achan's failure, God told them, "See, I have given into your hand the King of Ai and you shall do to him as you did to Jericho and its King. Only this time, you may take the treasure for yourselves." (Joshua 8:1, 2.) This is good news, but keep your sword and shield held high. *The Alliance*, awaits you, the second of the *Greater Temptations*, and possibly the toughest giant-battle of them all. You will be challenged like never before to "Hold fast to that which is good," (1 Thessalonians 5:21-28)

Giants In Detail 5
(The Alliance)

Therefore the five kings of the Amorites - gathered together and went up (against Israel) with all their armies.
Joshua 10:3–5

The Israelites defeated thirty-one wicked kings in their conquest of the promised land, but their battle with the *Alliance of the Five Kings* would decide whether they would go forward or die right there. These five kings (the King of Jerusalem, the King of Hebron, the King of Jarmuth, the King of Lachish, and the King of Eglon) represented the primary demonic forces that governed Canaan, and they are as strongly present in worldly culture today as they were back then. They assault a believer with the following temptations: Idolatry, nostalgia, covetousness, selfish ambition and validation. These are the greatest of the *Great Temptations*, and result in mighty downfalls when they are yielded to.

The danger lies in the fact that most Christians feel impervious to sin at this stage in the game. The devil is no newcomer, however, and initiates these temptations as soft scenes, dabbling in the dirt and tennis games with grace. Subtle beginnings that lead to spiritual trespasses.

Idolatry, for instance, is replacing God with something else. Nostalgia exalts a reverence for the past over Godly vision. Covetousness moves a soul from appreciating blessings to chasing them at any cost. Selfish ambition lifts purpose above love. And finally, validation displaces the foundation of self-worth in God with the druggy need for applause, accolades, and notoriety.

Do you see how easily these can creep in? This is how important this battle is: It is the only event mentioned in the entire Bible where God heeded the voice of a man and caused the sun to stand still until the wicked had been completely slaughtered. "There has been no day like it, before or after." (Joshua 10:14)

There will be no day like it in your life. You will go forward or stop right here. How do you get the victory? God will cause His light to stand still on your battle with these forces for however long it takes (He "floods the eyes of the heart with light." Ephesians 1:18), as long as you refuse to compromise with them. Stay in the light. Keep your conversations and activities in the light and, united though they might be, your foot will end up on these giant's necks. They are not your gods. They belong to the world.

I have faced all of these, and sure enough, they are joined elbow to elbow. Idolatry, nostalgia, covetousness, selfish ambition and validation—one flatters the other. In fact, flattery is their war cry. I found them difficult because the tiniest bit of success (as the small city of Ai was to the Israelites--an easy victory in the end), opens the door to them. Then, suddenly, the soul is bombarded with offers that are hard to say no to. How anchored are we? This is where we need to judge ourselves to avoid being judged (1 Corinthians 11:31). We live in these five kings' world—God has called us to it—but we are to bring culture to them, not adopt theirs. God says to you right now, "Do not fear them, for I have delivered them into your hand. Not one of them shall stand before you." (Joshua 10:8) For the Christian who withstands this test, the entire territory is open to him now. God's destiny lays before him. "So Joshua conquered all the land, the mountain country in the south and the low land and the wilderness slopes and all of their kings. He left none remaining." (Joshua: 10:41) So be it for you. May you walk the high hills of the earth with your God, undarkened by compromise and full of strength and vision. Amen.

The Isolation Tactics

Whoever isolates himself seeks his own desire; he breaks out against all sound judgment.
Proverbs 18:1

Have you noticed a lion, the ultimate predator, stalking its prey? It begins by charging into a herd, causing chaos and confusion. Amid the frenzy, the lion singles out one target—perhaps the weakest or the most vulnerable. It isolates this one from the herd, and once separated, the lion relentlessly pursues it until the inevitable, deadly capture. When the enemy seeks to destroy you, one of his most effective strategies is to isolate you. Proverbs 18:1 warns us, "Whoever isolates himself seeks his own desire; he breaks out against all sound judgment." Isolation can lead you down a dark path, one where selfish desires reign and wise counsel is ignored. It strips away the support and accountability that comes from being part of a community. Alone, you become an easy target for temptation and sin, much like the prey that has been separated from the herd.

Evil deeds thrive in isolation. Jesus tells us in John 3:19, 20 that "Light has come into the world, but people loved darkness instead of light because their deeds were evil." In the shadows, sin festers and grows, shielded from the exposing light of truth and community. When you isolate yourself, you step away from the illuminating power of fellowship and God's truth. This isolation allows sin to take root and flourish, unchallenged and unchecked. The Bible emphasizes the vital importance of community and mutual support. Hebrews 10:24, 25 urges believers, "And let us consider how we may spur one another on toward love and good deeds, not giving up meeting together, as some are in the habit of doing, but encouraging one another, and all the more as you see the Day approaching."

Also, people hurt themselves in isolation. Self-esteem and mental health can plummet. Some might seek solitude for rejuvenation, which is a different scenario entirely, but I'm trying to rouse your attention to the lure of the enemy when he orchestrates this isolation, creating an atmosphere of darkness. He wants to separate his intended prey from the herd, but in community there is strength. There is accountability. There is light. Don't allow yourself to be the isolated prey in the enemy's sights. Seek out fellowship, embrace the support of others, and stay within the protective circle of God's truth. Let your life be illuminated by the love and encouragement of your faith community. For in the light, darkness loses its power, and in unity, isolation loses its grip. Stay connected, stay supported, and let the light guide you away from the snares of isolation and sin.

Soul Gardens

The ruler of this world is coming, and he has nothing in me.
John 14:30

What was Jesus referring to when He told His disciples in John 14:30 that the devil had nothing in Him? Did He think of Himself as a sort of spirit hotel with a *no vacancy* sign up? According to the description of the temple described in Ezekiel 40, that picture is not far off,. It discloses some fascinating secrets. Here we find that God's temple mirrors the blueprint of a human soul, which has an outer wall comprised of thirty rooms. I thought that thirty might be a metaphor, so I checked, and sure enough, psychology tells us that there are thirty different personality traits that can be categorized under five main types. So, now we understand that a human soul is divided into a complex series of rooms (or sections), and that each room holds a particular soil. Both God and the devil have seeds that they would like to sow in them. For instance, if you were taught about Jesus from your childhood, the soil in the garden room called *faith* would be rich and deep and it would be difficult for someone to uproot its plantings. If you were traumatized emotionally somewhere along the line, the soil in your *trust* room might be thick with patches of doubt and wariness. The rest of you might be fine, but the devil has something in your *trust* room. Ideas, values, order and compassion—these are the names of some of our other rooms, and they all contribute to the state of our soul.

Now we understand Matthew 13 better, and the parable of the sower. The exposed ground, the rocky ground, the thorny ground and the good ground. The soils of our various soul rooms are all going to fall into one of these categories. And here's another truth: just as God's word needs good soil to flourish in, so does the devil's.

The devil's lies do no better on rocky or thorny ground than God's Word does. Isn't that fascinating? A stubborn, stuff-necked, rocky- soil man is about as useless to the devil as he is to God, except to raise a ruckus perhaps. He doesn't listen to anybody, doesn't believe anything, nor does he contribute anything to the world but complaints. But, if the devil can take over the good soil in a room and create a stronghold, he has a place to operate from.

I first understood this when years ago a friend explained to me that a stronghold is not a demon, but is a demonically-inspired belief system. I'll share an example from personal experience: I met a Christian woman once whose *trust* room had been violated through a series of traumas that occurred when she was a child. The damage was significant. In every other area, she was charming, intelligent, and full of energy, but when something triggered her memories, the emotions unleashed caused her to fly into an uncontrollable rage. Her very countenance changed.

When I asked God about this, He showed me that a demon was going to-and-fro through a small trap door in the woman's soul. It had a room. When the circumstances were right, the demon would torment the woman for a time and then leave. "Why is it still there after all these years?" I asked. "Because she's comfortable with it," God said.

It's important to understand that although we can bind demons from afflicting people, the strongholds themselves can't be prayed away, praised away, or cast out. They must be pulled down, (2 Corinthians 10:4), and replaced by the truth through meditating on God's Word.

John 8:32 tells us, "You shall know the truth and the truth will set you free." There is another great scripture, "He who keeps his way preserves his soul." (Proverbs 16:17) Jesus practiced this. Even the assault on His mind in Gethsemane couldn't pierce Him because His walls were strong, and His soils were pure. He had never believed a lie. The devil had nothing in Him.

Faith, Strength, and Weakness

After overcoming strongholds, believers are
reminded that they must rely on God's strength,
especially in times of weakness. These are
insights into faith and dependence on God.

Binding God

So my word be that goes forth from my mouth; it shall not return to me unfulfilled, but will accomplish that which pleases me and will prosper in that thing for which I sent it.
Isaiah 55:1

Once God has prophesied something over your life and you have agreed to it, you have bound God to His own faithfulness. At any point after that, you might decide to run like Jonah, disobey like Saul, deny like Peter, or doubt like Thomas, but all your efforts at canceling the contract will only bring unnecessary pressure to the situation. You can zig-zag if you want to, but God is still moving in a straight line. He has to. His Word can't return void. So, when you don't get the job you applied for, aren't able to successfully relocate yourself, or find yourself standing alone where there once was a loyal alliance, don't be surprised. You are not your own anymore. You belong to God and His plan for you, and He is now the architect of your journey, which always seems unforgivingly narrow as He steadfastly guides you to your prophetic destination.

Think about Mary. Mary said yes to the angel of God about conceiving a child and from that point on, she and Joseph couldn't come and go as they pleased. God's faithfulness was alive in the atmosphere and His hands were involved in every situation as they dodged the enemy's attempts to abort the promise. For, every promise has an enemy. Every prophecy has been publicly trumpeted, and the devil is quick to mobilize his demonic resources against them.

About fifteen years ago, I began to grow impatient with God, especially concerning my finances in relation to the things I felt He had called me to do. I made a list, at the top of which were these two things, written just this way: 1. Look for jobs. 2. Look for money.

The following Saturday I went to a prayer meeting, and after a time of worship, we were all invited to leave our seats and pray as we were led. I was standing in the center of the room with my eyes closed and my arms at my sides when a woman I barely knew grabbed me in a bear hug and pressed her lips directly against one of my ears. "Don't look for jobs and don't look for money," she whispered. "I will lead you every step of the way." Then she released me and walked away to pray with someone else. That got my attention. She had spoken out verbatim the very same words I had written down just days before. When I got home, I crumpled up the list I had made and redirected my focus on the things that were directly in front of me. I left my money concerns in God's hands. He is my provider.

I've been in the whale's belly before. I have run away like Jonah, doubted like Thomas, denied like Peter, and disobeyed like David; but none of my failings have canceled God's promises to me or weakened the prophetic strength of His declarations. His power to perform His Word was hanging over every step I took.

Remember that God's character is faithfulness. He is not a man that He should lie, nor a human being that is fickle and changes his mind. (Numbers 23:19). If He said it, it will come to pass. If He told you something and you said yes to it, you have bound Him to His promise and He will not fail you.

Stay Simple

My strength is made perfect in weakness.
2 Corinthians 12:9

I was fortunate enough to attend some meetings held by a fairly well-known healing evangelist some years ago. The meetings were small, less than 100 people, and it was a privilege to listen to this wise man of God teach about God's healing power in an intimate setting. I scribbled down some notes on the inside of my Bible's cover that are still there to this day. The highlights amounted to this: "If we are called upon to pray for someone who needs healing, we are not to doubt whether or not we are spiritually ready for the assignment. Have we been fasting and praying lately? It doesn't matter. The power of God is already present to heal through the Holy Spirit who lives within us." In other words, if we are called upon, we just need to go. This is why a minister with a secret can still do God's business. So can a new believer with no experience. To think otherwise is to believe that some labor on our part is necessary.

To illustrate this, here's a true story: In 1997, my children's grandmother on their mother's side moved from Reno to Tulsa to be closer to them. Her heart was in the right place, but it was difficult for her because she suffered from migraines to the point where she often couldn't get out of bed. The doctors gave her shots, but all they did was take the edge off. I watched this for a while, the terrible suffering, until I couldn't stand to see it go on any longer. But I was still young in my walk with the Lord. What should I do? Tentatively, I asked Grandma if I could pray for her one morning and she said yes. She sat down on the living room sofa without a shred of faith in her eyes and I laid hands on her. "Be healed in Jesus' name!" I said. Instantly, I felt something move between us and she stared up at me with wide, blinking eyes. "It's gone!" She's never had another migraine and it's been thirty years.

I often remind myself of Grandma's healing. The incident was so spontaneous, there wasn't time for doubt to flash across my mind. It's a good reminder to stay simple concerning God's power. It's not our strength or energy that does the work. It's His. Our only job is to reach out the hand. Then, if the receiver is open, the power is there to get the job done. If nothing happens, it isn't our concern. God knows all about the situation.

Fearful Hunches, Faithless Actions

We seemed like grasshoppers in our own eyes, and we looked the same to them.
Numbers 13:33

Imagine a man standing at the edge of a vast chasm, paralyzed by the fear of crossing. He's convinced himself that the bridge before him is too fragile, despite it being sturdy and well-constructed. His fear poisons his mind with lies, leading him to either stand still, rooted in inaction, or to make reckless attempts to cross elsewhere. I know the feeling. When I was young, I dabbled in the arts and made greeting cards, wrote short stories and drew pictures, but I was also great at physics, mathematics, and chemistry. These were my favorite subjects, in fact. I was very smart, but I had one fear—the fear of failure. I would never attempt something I wasn't sure I would excel at. I was afraid of embarrassing myself.

Fear can twist our perceptions and justify our unwise decisions. It can make us falter and turn away from the path laid out for us, leading to poor choices. Take Peter, for example. In Matthew 14:29-31, Peter steps out of the boat and walks on the water toward Jesus. What an accomplishment! He started out strong, but the moment he notices the wind and the waves, fear grips him and he begins to sink. Jesus catches him, but admonishes him with a stinging rebuke. "You of little faith, why did you doubt?"

Our fearful hunches can cause us to falter if we lose sight of Christ, the focus of our faith. Consider the Israelites in Numbers 13:31-33. After spying out the promised land, the sight of the giants caused them to be consumed by fear. Despite God's promise to be with them, they fixated on the formidable inhabitants of the land and their own perceived inadequacies, saying, "We seemed like grasshoppers in our own eyes, and we looked the same to them." Their fear led them to rebel against God's plan, resulting in 40 years of wandering in the wilderness. The repercussions were severe.

These stories highlight a critical truth: fear can lead us to act faithlessly and justify our actions based on practicality or realism rather than God's assurances. However, this mindset can steer us away from God's will. Isaiah 41:10 offers a powerful counter to fear-based thinking: "Do not fear, for I am with you; do not be dismayed, for I am your God. I will strengthen you and help you; I will uphold you with my righteous right hand." This verse reassures us of God's constant presence and support, even when circumstances seem daunting.

Examine the motivations behind your actions. Are you avoiding a step of faith because you're afraid of failure? Are you making decisions based on a desire to control your outcomes rather than trusting in God's plan for you? Remember that Jesus has promised to never leave your side. Resist fear and you will avoid the pitfalls of faithless decisions and walk the path that God has set before you.

The Sticky Anointing

God did extraordinary miracles through Paul.
Acts 19:11

There is a healing anointing from God that sticks to inanimate objects similar to the way radiation does. It has a spiritual half-life that allows power to remain long after its initial application. The apostle Paul experienced this phenomenon. Acts 19:12 tells us that "handkerchiefs and aprons that touched him were taken to the sick, and their illnesses were cured, and the evil spirits left them." The important thing to see is that as the handkerchiefs and aprons traveled from Paul to their destination, time did not diminish the power attached to them.

I have a friend whose son ended up in a mental institution. When she was praying about the situation, God told her, "Buy a shirt for him and lay hands on it. Then send it to him." She followed the instructions and when the young man received the package in the mail and put the shirt on, he came to his right mind immediately. The power attached to the garment had not diminished in transit.

This startling early-church type of deliverance took place not many years ago in the New York City area, only in this case, the item wasn't a handkerchief or an apron but was a menswear item from a department store in the mall. Anything will do. I should also mention that the lady in question was a lay person, not a preacher. She had no great ministry. She just heard God's voice and obeyed.

When we hear of such things, our tendency is to examine the details too closely. "God must need to use fabric." But atoms are all the same to God and He could just as easily use a rock, a suitcase, or a bicycle to heal someone. Do you have the faith for it? Here is a story: In 2 Kings 13 we are told that a dead man's body was thrown into a tomb containing Elisha's bones. Immediately the dead man came to life and stood to his feet. There was power in those bones! In all likelihood, this is the reason why God hid Moses' body in the desert and why Satan argued with the archangel Michael so vehemently about the issue. (Jude 1:9) Perhaps part of God remained attached to Moses and Satan wanted to capitalize on the fact. How, we just don't know.

I have this much faith: I've played the same guitar in thousands of worship services, and I feel like part of God is stuck to it. I won't part with it. I also own a Bible whose pages have been handled by an angel (I'll discuss this in another article), and an ornate jacket that God gave to me as a gift. I call it my "God Jacket." I haven't seen God face-to-face like Moses, and I haven't walked in the power of Elisha, but I've been in God's presence enough to believe that some of His anointing has adhered to me and at least a few of my possessions. When my children inherit them, something will be passed along. Healing power maybe, or even just a quickening to love righteousness. It's up to God. They are just things, but I have the faith for it.

Our Will and God's Ability

"If you are willing, you can make me clean." Jesus, moved with compassion, replied, "I am willing," and healed him.
Matthew 8:2, 3

Connecting willingness to ability is essential in overcoming life's challenges. It's one thing to have the desire to accomplish something and another entirely to possess the means to achieve it. This truth is particularly profound when we face our limitations and weaknesses. Every day, we confront the reality that, even at our best, we are finite beings. This realization can lead to a sense of learned helplessness, knowing that there is only so much we can do in our own strength. However, as believers in Christ Jesus, we have access to a power beyond any limitations. This divine connection aligns our willingness with God's infinite ability.

Imagine being in a dark, empty room with no way out. You might be willing to leave, but without light or a guide, your willingness alone isn't enough. Similarly, in life, our willingness needs to be coupled with God's unlimited ability. The Bible gives us a clear example of this in the story of the man with leprosy who approached Jesus. He said, "If you are willing, you can make me clean." Jesus, moved with compassion, replied, "I am willing," and healed him. (Matthew 8:2, 3). The leper had been living in his own dark, empty room of sickness, full of doubt, perhaps, but God was both willing and able to help him.

God is available in the same way when our willingness meets the stubborn obstacle of our inability to effect change in our lives. This requires trust and patience. Eventually, an instruction will come, and if we rise to do our part without hesitancy, the entire landscape around us will change. The Bible reminds us, "If you are willing and obedient, you will eat the good things of the land." (Isaiah 1:19) Abundance and blessings are on the other side of action.

When confronted with our limitations and weaknesses, we should remember that God is infinite, and His ability knows no bounds. With strong faith and by aligning our willingness with God's ability, we can experience miracles and wonders. It's not just about believing in God's power but trusting in His willingness to use that power for our good. In doing so, we open the door to a life marked by divine intervention, extraordinary breakthroughs, and a deeper connection with the One who holds the universe in His hands.

Living Dogs and Dead Lions

For a living dog is better than a dead lion.
Ecclesiastes 9:4

I am old enough now to have encountered both living dogs and dead lions in my life. I knew a *lion* once, a former prizefighter who had at some point become a Christian and started his own business. I watched him grow in the Holy Spirit over the years to the point where he would hear an instruction from the Lord and obey it instantly. What a fruitful partnership he had with God! Every move he made brought him increase. Finally, there came a time when he went from poverty status to millionaire status over the period of a single winter, enabling him to purchase a beautiful house in a picturesque, south Tulsa neighborhood. Then pride got in.

He started to believe that God would bless any decision he made, leading to some bad investments that cost him everything. Next, he became ill. A simple operation would have saved his life, but he was adamant about receiving his healing by faith. I respected that, but faith and wisdom are partners. Sometimes God performs miracles, sometimes He uses doctors. In any case, the man grew weaker and weaker. The last time I saw him I urged him to let me take him to the hospital, but his answer was a firm, rebuking no. "I'm going to receive my healing by faith, and I don't want to hear another word about it!" Two weeks later he was found dead in his bed. He had been a genuine lion of the faith, I can attest to that, but in a season of setbacks he didn't have the humility to accept the help that was offered to him.

Around that same time, I knew a *dog*—an unbeliever who had been diagnosed with throat cancer. Out of desperation, he started attending church and developed a sort of weak, wavering faith, but he kept on smoking his cigarettes and drinking his beer and his condition grew worse. In time, his treatments failed, and he was sent to a nursing home to die. I was there when the doctors told him "Get your affairs in order because the cancer has spread to all the rest of your organs." After the doctors left the room, I prayed for him, but I didn't think I would ever see him again. To my surprise, he called me two weeks later from an apartment he had rented. He had walked out of the nursing home on his own and had no intentions of ever going back. What happened? I think that his tiny, childlike faith had been enough. There was no pride blocking the way and God's power had found an unobstructed avenue to flow through.

The lesson is fairly simple. Pride contaminates our faith and gets in God's way. The great healing evangelist Smith Wigglesworth used to say, "The grape is always the ripest right before it begins to rot." It's true. As believers, the time to be on guard is when our faith is at its strongest. We might be tempted to take some of the credit for our successes. We might even begin to have faith in our faith, which is not the same thing as having faith in God. It's a subtle deception. Whatever it takes, we need to stay alive. There is work to be done, and a living dog still has the potential to become a lion, whereas the journey of a dead lion is over.

The Power Paradox

Samson said, "Let me die with the Philistines!" Then he pushed with all his might, and down came the temple on the rulers and all the people in it. Thus he killed many more when he died than while he lived.
Judges 16:30

The Christian life has nothing to do with being strong or tough; wisdom is the more supreme characteristic. King Solomon, with all his splendor, wasn't a warrior brandishing swords or brawling in the heat of battle. No, his weapon was wisdom, and with it he amassed treasures and respect beyond measure. Imagine it! King Solomon's power stemmed not from the bloodshed of war but from the profound depths of his mind. His reign was marked by peace and prosperity, a display of the triumph of wisdom over brute force.

In contrast, there's Samson—a tragic figure, a man of immense physical power but sorely lacking in wisdom and discipline. His is a tale of what happens when strength is unbridled and untempered by insight. Samson's feats of strength were legendary, tearing lions apart with his bare hands, slaying thousands with the jawbone of a donkey, but what good was all that might when his mind was clouded by folly? His downfall was a slow unraveling, led by his fleshly desires, and his trust in the untrustworthy. He revealed the secret of his strength to Delilah, and in his vulnerability, he was betrayed. She cut his hair and the Philistines captured him, gouged out his eyes, and bound him in chains.

His final act was one of sheer brute force, collapsing a temple and killing himself along with his captors, a victory tainted with the bitterness of humiliation and loss. Judges 16:30 tells us, "Samson said, 'Let me die with the Philistines!' Then he pushed with all his might, and down came the temple on the rulers and all the people in it. Thus he killed many more when he died than while he lived." It didn't have to end that way, though.

In comparison, Solomon's end was serene. A king revered and honored, his wisdom echoed through generations. Proverbs 4:7 says, "Wisdom is the principal thing; therefore get wisdom: and with all thy getting get understanding." Strength might shatter bones, but wisdom builds empires. Physical strength, without the guiding hand of wisdom, becomes a curse, a destructive force that can lead to a man's ruin. Samson's life was a storm of violence and passion, ending in a death as brutal as his exploits. Solomon's life was a testament to the power of a discerning mind, his influence extending far beyond his reign.

It's not the muscles that make a man mighty; it's the mind, and the wisdom in it that guides his actions. Strength is but a tool, and in the hands of the wise, it can build wonders. But in the hands of the foolish, it will only bring about their downfall. Choose wisdom, and you choose a legacy that endures.

Release Brings Relief

Come to me, all you who are weary and burdened, and I will give you rest. Take my yoke upon you and learn from me, for I am gentle and humble in heart, and you will find rest for your souls. For my yoke is easy and my burden is light.
Matthew 11:28-30

Life often feels like we're trudging through a dense, shadowy forest, dragging along chains of worry and challenges. Yet, even in the darkest moments, Jesus offers a profound promise: "Come to me, all you who are weary and burdened, and I will give you rest." (Matthew 11:28-30) Rest is achieved by handing over our worries and burdens to God. Think of Moses, who handed over his staff—a simple piece of wood—only for it to become a tool of miracles. He would go on to part the Red Sea, bring forth water from a rock, and turn the Nile River into blood with it. When we release our burdens, God will work wonders in our lives too. He will turn our burdens into power conductors, but first we must release the following: control, resentment, self-reliance, anxiety, guilt and fear. These five things. Let's examine them:

☐ *Control:* Relinquishing control doesn't mean giving up completely, it means trusting God with the reins. Proverbs 3:5, 6 advises, "Trust in the Lord with all your heart and lean not on your own understanding; in all your ways submit to him, and he will make your paths straight." When we let go of the need to control every detail, we make room for God's perfect plan to unfold.

☐ *Resentment and Bitterness:* These two emotions are like chains that bind our heart, preventing us from experiencing true peace. Ephesians 4:31, 32 urges us to "Get rid of all bitterness, rage and anger, brawling and slander, along with every form of malice. Be kind and compassionate to one another, forgiving each other, just as in Christ God forgave you." Forgiveness breaks the chains and frees our soul from the poisons of resentment and bitterness.

☐ *Self-Reliance:* While it's important to work hard and be responsible, relying solely on our own strength can lead to burnout. Trust in God's power and provision. As Paul reminds us in 2 Corinthians 12:9, "My grace is sufficient for you, for my power is made perfect in weakness." We need to acknowledge our limits and let God's strength fill in the gaps.

☐ *Anxiety and Stress:* Life is full of situations that can trigger anxiety, but Jesus offers us a peace that surpasses all understanding. Philippians 4:6, 7 encourages us, "Do not be anxious about anything, but in every situation, by prayer and petition, with thanksgiving, present your requests to God. And the peace of God, which transcends all understanding, will guard your hearts and your minds in Christ Jesus." This divine peace is like a fortress for our mind and heart.

☐ *Guilt and Shame:* The weight of guilt can be crushing, but Jesus lifts that burden through His sacrifice. 1 John 1:9 assures us, "If we confess our sins, he is faithful and just and will forgive us our sins and purify us from all unrighteousness." When we lay our guilt at the foot of the cross, we will receive forgiveness and a clean slate.

☐ *Fear of the Future:* The unknown can be terrifying, but trusting in God's plans for us brings a profound sense of security. Jeremiah 29:11 offers a promise: "For I know the plans I have for you, declares the Lord, plans to prosper you and not to harm you, plans to give you hope and a future." When we trust in God's plan, we become hopeful of the future, not fearful. To experience this divine relief, we must connect with Jesus on a deep, personal level.

Release your burdens and trust in God's love and guidance. As you surrender and align yourself with His will, you will discover the peace, comfort, and freedom that only He can provide. Let go of your burdens, embrace His yoke, and find rest for your soul.

The Source of Your Strength

By faith, these people overthrew kingdoms, ruled with justice, and received what God had promised them... Their weakness was turned to strength
Hebrews 11:33, 34

Growing up, I was the sharp kid—quick with words, clever, and not shy about showing it. Every now and then, I'd strut around with my ego a little larger than life. But one memory from when I was eleven or twelve still burns. I had boldly challenged my uncle to a spelling bee and nailed all my words effortlessly until he threw out a new one: "philosophy." Confidently, I spelled it "filosofy." I had to be right. How could a word with the "f" sound start with "ph"? My uncle declared that I was wrong, however, and my siblings gathered around as I stormed off to grab my pocket dictionary. And there it was: "philosophy."

The word glared back at me in all its correct syntax, exposing my mistake. The shame hit hard. I had been so bullishly wrong, so convinced I was right, only to have reality slap me in the face. I shrank back to my room, fighting tears, and vowed to make the dictionary my new best friend. That moment taught me more than just spelling—it showed me how foolish it is to place my confidence in myself.

Life's battles are fierce, and it's natural to lean on what we have—our skills, our friends, our savings—but these are not our ultimate sources of strength. The true power lies in trusting God, who alone can deliver and sustain us through every trial. Take King David for example. He decided to count his soldiers, believing that sheer numbers would ensure victory, but this act of self-reliance displeased God and led to serious consequences. David realized his error and confessed, "I have sinned greatly by doing this. Please take away my guilt, for I have done a foolish thing" (2 Samuel 24:10). His misstep illustrates a vital lesson: relying on our own resources rather than on God's strength can lead to downfall.

Now, picture Gideon, who led a mere 300 men against a massive army. The odds were stacked against him, but the victory was secured by God's power. Gideon's story echoes a truth found in Hebrews 11:33, 34: "By faith, these people overthrew kingdoms, ruled with justice, and received what God had promised them." Gideon's triumph reminds us that faith in God can achieve the impossible. Here's how you can apply this to your life:

- ☐ *Daily Trust:* Start each day by leaning on God. Begin with a prayer, asking for His guidance and strength. Proverbs 3:5, 6 encourages us, "Trust in the Lord with all your heart and lean not on your own understanding; in all your ways submit to Him, and He will make your paths straight."
- ☐ *Scripture Meditation:* Fill your mind with verses that remind you of God's strength. Isaiah 40:31 promises, "But those who hope in the Lord will renew their strength. They will soar on wings like eagles; they will run and not grow weary; they will walk and not be faint." Let these words fortify your spirit.
- ☐ *Faith in Action:* Demonstrate your trust in God through bold steps of faith. Even when circumstances look bleak, remember Philippians 4:13: "I can do all this through Him who gives me strength." With God's power, you are equipped to face any challenge.

Now, reflect on your current struggles. Are you relying on your own abilities, or are you placing your trust in God? Like David and Gideon, your true strength and victory must come from Him. Watch as He transforms your weaknesses into strengths. Charles Spurgeon wisely said, "We are too prone to engrave our trials in marble and write our blessings in sand." Let's reverse that. Let's engrave our trust in marble and let the sands of yesterday bury our trials. God is the true source of our strength. When we anchor our hope in Him, we don't just survive, we thrive.

What You Heard in The Beginning

Therefore let that abide in you which you heard in the beginning.
1 John 2:24

Time will not exist in Heaven. But here on earth, every event in a human life has a beginning, a middle and an end, and God is present in each of them. Even more importantly, He will inform you of where He is taking you, why you are going there, and what the outcome will be—all in advance.

Do you doubt this? Let me remind you that God warned the Israelites over and over again that they would soon be dragged away in chains to Babylon. He told them how they would get there, how long their stay would be, and when they would return. This was God interacting prophetically with the Israelites and He interacts with us in very much the same way.

The "things that we hear in the beginning" of a situation are given to keep us encouraged when the journey seems to be more challenging than we can bear. The devil shouts, "Now you've done it, you're heading nowhere," while God's Word reminds us that there is always a return from exile as promised. But clouds of gloom still surround our heads occasionally. "If only I could see it from God's perspective," we think, and we can.

Ezekiel 1 will help us. Here we are shown the spiritual machinery of God's creation—the engineering behind the scenes: "The appearance of their workings was, as it were, a wheel in the middle of a wheel." The outer wheel mentioned here is time, and the inner wheel is a picture of the generations of individual lives that populate it. It's a picture of human history, you and I included, and God sits at the center of it all. He will reveal what He wants, when He wants, and to whomever He wants, as He sees fit. And because He sees the past, present and future simultaneously, we don't have to worry that our behavior somewhere along the line will cancel out something that He has guaranteed us. He has taken everything into account. So hold on to what He says to you. Your history will play out just as He has described.

There is another aspect to this *"time-is-a-wheel"* idea. In numbers 11:23, God rebuked Moses for his unbelief and said to him, "Has my arm been shortened? Now you will see whether or not my word comes true." Moses was experiencing a universal difficulty. He was finding it difficult to believe something God had told him when the circumstances were looking contrary. But God was trying to teach Moses some spiritual geometry: "The length of my arm is the distance from my throne to the earth. I can touch any point in history because I sit at the spoke. It is all the same distance to me." To suggest that the future is out of God's reach does Him a great disservice. In fact, He designed this geometry with us in mind. He doesn't have to stretch to insert Himself in our lives.

You may be in a difficult place right now, but don't be surprised. In Genesis 15:12, Moses fell into a deep sleep just after God told him his future and "a thick and dreadful darkness came over him." This is the shadow of the time wheel---*the valley of the shadow of death*—and we all experience it. In that momentary confusion, hold on to what you heard in the beginning. You are in the womb of your prophetic future, protected from the enemy for a time, and when you emerge, your life will look exactly like He has said.

Your Soul Hangs in The Balance

Be sober, be vigilant; because your adversary the devil walks about like a roaring lion, seeking whom he may devour.
1 Peter 5:8

Growing up in northern Nigeria, where the population is predominantly Muslim, Christians often face persecution. In the area where my family planted its first church, a neighbor practiced black magic. Though we didn't know this initially, his activities were well-known in the neighborhood. However, as our ministry's presence affected his powers, he attempted to cast a spell on the church. The spell backfired, and he fell ill. Out of desperation, he asked for my mother, known for her strong prayer lifestyle, to come pray for him. When she visited, he confessed what he had tried to do, and they prayed together. He died a premature death not long after. Truly, as the Bible says, "No weapon formed against you shall prosper, and every tongue that rises against you in judgment is condemned." (Isaiah 54:17) The Lord watches over His own.

Rebellion against God always brings destruction. Historians have written extensively about the fall of Jerusalem, painting the scenes with bloody strokes. It was a nightmare made real: men, women, young, old—none were spared. Henry Hart Milman, in *The History of the Jews*, describes this: "The slaughter within was even more dreadful than the spectacle from without. Men and women, old and young, insurgents and priests, those who fought and those who entreated mercy, were hewn down in indiscriminate carnage." Josephus also wrote of these horrors, offering an eyewitness account that chills the blood even centuries later.

The fall of Jerusalem was a historical tragedy and a manifestation of Satan's vindictive power over those who yield to his control. This was the culmination of warnings ignored, a crescendo of disobedience. God had repeatedly urged Israel to turn away from idolatry and sin, but they chose the seductive sway of the enemy over the clarion call of the Almighty. He would like to inflict the same damage on us. He'll lie, tempt, manipulate, frustrate—anything to lead us astray. The warnings of the Apostle Peter in 1 Peter 5:8 are not a metaphor: "Be sober, be vigilant; because your adversary the devil walks about like a roaring lion, seeking whom he may devour."

The enemy's hunger is insatiable, his malice unending. He thrives on destruction, relishing the fall of each soul into despair. We should not just strive to survive the enemy's onslaught but strive to thrive in the light of Christ. We must recognize the battle for what it is—an immense struggle between good and evil, with our souls hanging in the balance. Don't be a passive participant in this saga. Arm yourself with faith, gird yourself with the Word, and stand firm. The enemy may be a fearsome adversary, but with Christ, you have a champion who has already won the war.

Wisdom, Discernment, and Revelation

Once we draw strength from God, the next step is cultivating wisdom and discernment—vital tools for walking closely with Him and applying His Word in our daily lives. Through this process, we gain deeper revelation and a clearer understanding of God's nature and His essence.

Absolute Truth

You shall know the truth and the truth shall set you free.
John 8:32

Truth is a concept that feels both solid and slippery at the same time. We think we have a grasp on it, then it slides out of our hands like a greased eel. But let's not kid ourselves—truth is more than a whimsical concept conjured by philosophers. Truth is consistent, agrees with the facts, and is loyal. But in this world of shadows and shifting sands, how do we pin it down?

Imagine four types of truth. Each is a creature of its own kind, stalking the landscape of our minds.

First, there's *objective truth*, the bedrock of reality. These are the proven physical realities that surround our existence. The sun rises in the east, gravity pulls us to the ground, and water is wet. No debate, no argument.

Next, we have *normative truth*. These are truths agreed upon by groups. In English speaking countries, we call the bright part of a 24-hour cycle *day*. We all agree upon this. It's a social contract, a handshake agreement.

Then there's *subjective truth*. This one is trickier, and more personal. It's your truth, my truth, their truth. For instance, "Today is a good day" might be true for some, but it isn't for everyone. It has to do with our personal experiences and perspectives.

Finally, there's *complex truth*, the synthesis of all truths. Complex truth combines objective, normative, and subjective truths together, creating a coherent picture out of disparate threads.

How do we navigate all of these conflicting narratives? Well, let's consider a fifth and higher concept, *Absolute Truth*. This is the truth that stands tall in all circumstances. "There is no such thing as a round square." It's the truth that remains when all the illusions have been stripped away. Denying absolute truth often means denying accountability, skirting the edges of chaos. Consider the evidence for absolute truth. First, there is the human conscience, our innate sense of right and wrong. It is the calm inner voice that nudges us away from the abyss. Then there's science, the cold, hard facts that stand unbowed in the face of opinion. And finally, there's religion. It provides meaning, connection, and divine explanations for all of existence. Absolute truth points to something beyond the veil, a sovereign God who desires a personal relationship with us through Jesus Christ. As John 8:32 says, "You shall know the truth and the truth shall set you free."

Why should we arm ourselves with the truth? For freedom! Freedom from the identity crisis that gnaws at our core. We need to root our identity in the unchanging image of God, not in the fickle reflections of society, which are evident in subjective truth. Avoid being swayed by these stormy whispers. Renew your mind with God's truth, as Romans 12:2 advises, and let it be your anchor. Read the Word of God and wield it like a sword. Apply it to your life, and feel it strengthen and steady you. It's more than just knowledge, it's a living, breathing transformative power that will bring a metamorphosis to your soul. The truth is always there, waiting for you to grasp it. It's a beacon in the fog, a lighthouse in the storm. Seek it, embrace it, and let it set you free.

Two Kinds of Light

…The things which are seen were not made of things which are visible.
Hebrews 11:3

There are two kinds of light: *eternal light* and *created light*. Eternal light has always existed and has properties that can't be measured. Created light was made specifically for this creation when God said, "Let there be light," and has limited properties that can be divided into three measurable categories: visible light, infrared light and ultraviolet light. Being limited to those wavelengths, it is a weak power that cannot make visible everything that exists. Beings are coming and going around us all of the time, but the powers of the sun, the moon, and manmade light don't expose them. Since we only see a fraction of what exists, the following becomes a pillar: "By faith we understand that the universe was created by the word of God, so that what is seen was not made out of things that are visible." (Hebrews 11:3)

Conversely, our lives are lived in full view of the spiritual world. We are as bright as stars to anybody who cares to look, be they angel or demon. The Word of God affirms this when it declares, "Each one appears before God in Zion," in Psalm 84:7. This scripture is referring to the children of God and it reveals that every moment of our lives is lived in front of His eyes like a film played in slow motion. Even those in the great cloud of witnesses are able to watch us to a limited degree. It seems a bit unfair, doesn't it? We only perceive created light and the atoms and molecules it illuminates, but the stage we come and go on is bathed in eternal light. But the design has purpose. God foresaw our dilemma and gave us a sixth sense called *faith*. We are creatures with six senses, not five. We are told in Hebrews 11:1 that Faith detects substances we can't see, making faith the spiritual hand that we use to interact beyond the spectrums of created light. It can touch God's throne, which can't be seen, and curse a fig tree which can be seen, with equal ease. It can command an unclean spirit to leave, which can't be seen, and command a dead body to rise, which can be seen, in a single motion. Faith operates in both eternal light and created light and is a power that the devil and his hosts don't possess.

You thought you were handicapped, but your weakness is actually your strength! Your hand of faith is as long as God's arm, which has no limits, so when you move to utilize it, ignore the sights and situations that surround you. They are merely the perceptions of your natural eye and will distract you. Focus on what your faith detects, the substance of the things you're hoping for, and the Father of Lights (eternal light and created light both), will meet you in power on the other side of the dark glass. Nothing will be impossible to you.

Eternity In Our Hearts

He has made everything beautiful in its time. He has also set eternity in the human heart,
yet no one can fathom what God has done from beginning to end.
Ecclesiastes 3:11

I grew up listening to the Irish boy-band Westlife. Their music, filled with heartfelt lyrics and emotive melodies, left an indelible mark on my teenage years. I could sing nearly all of their songs from memory, with exact precision in dynamic arrangements, pauses, breaks, and vocal inflections. One of my favorite songs, "Flying Without Wings," contains a line that speaks a profound truth: "Everybody's looking for that something. One thing that makes it all complete." Throughout the song, the band suggests various things, people, and places, where this *something* might be found, all connected by one thread—relationships. Relationships are indeed the most fundamentally important aspects of our lives.

Without relationships, life has no meaning. Things are defined based on their relationship with other things, whether geographical, dimensional, functional, or material. For human beings, our associations and networks with one another are significant, but they pale in comparison to our relationship with our Creator. When this vertical relationship is not firm, we feel lost, disoriented, purposeless, and incomplete.

There's a reason for this. It's often said, "There's a God-sized hole in our hearts that only He can fill." And it's true. Anything else we try to put in this hole leaves us empty and wanting. Ecclesiastes 3:11 tells us, "He has made everything beautiful in its time. He has also set eternity in the human heart, yet no one can fathom what God has done from beginning to end." The statement "He has also set eternity in the human heart," implies that humans have an innate sense of the eternal. We all want to be remembered, to leave a legacy, to have something that keeps us alive long after we're gone. This deepest longing in our hearts is a reflection of our desire for eternity.

As believers, we understand that our relationship with God determines how we will spend eternity. It won't matter what the world thinks of us as long as God recognizes us as His own when we stand before Him on Judgment day. The Bible emphasizes the importance of understanding how our lives here on earth play a part in our eternal destination. In Matthew 6:19-21, Jesus says, "Do not store up for yourselves treasures on earth, where moths and vermin destroy, and where thieves break in and steal. But store up for yourselves treasures in heaven, where moths and vermin do not destroy, and where thieves do not break in and steal. For where your treasure is, there your heart will be also." This reminds us that our earthly pursuits and relationships should align with our eternal goals. When we focus on building that crucial relationship with our Creator and fill that God-sized hole with His presence, we will find purpose and satisfy the longing for eternity that He has placed in our hearts.

Revelation, Not Information

I keep asking that the God of our Lord Jesus Christ, the glorious Father, may give you
the Spirit of wisdom and revelation, so that you may know him better
Ephesians 1:17

When I was a teenager in Nigeria, I was very active in my church. I led worship, played the drums and preached even. I was seventeen when I delivered my first Sunday morning sermon in front of the main congregation, and although it was nerve wracking, I could sense God's presence and hand on me. I've always felt close to God, but for a long time I wasn't sure which path I was to follow. Should I be a musician? A pastor? I knew His Word and was confident that I belonged to Him, but to be honest, I had never really pressed in to hear His voice concerning the more detailed aspects of His plan for me. When I did, I began to get clearer direction. Revelation began to come.

When God gives us revelation, He's addressing more than just our present self, He's speaking to the person He has destined us to become. His revelations are always prophetic, always future directed, pushing the potential He has planted within us forward. The result is the ignition of a transformative process fundamental to victorious living.

Paul's prayer captures this in Ephesians 1:17, 18. "I keep asking that the God of our Lord Jesus Christ, the glorious Father, may give you the Spirit of wisdom and revelation, so that you may know him better," he wrote. "I pray that the eyes of your heart may be enlightened so that you may know the hope to which he has called you, the riches of his glorious inheritance in his holy people." This type of revelation surpasses information. It involves an enlightenment that penetrates the soul and provides details for successful living.

Consider Jeremiah 29:11, where God says, "For I know the plans I have for you. Plans to prosper you and not to harm you, plans to give you hope and a future." God is speaking to the people He envisions us to be—strong, faithful individuals who align ourselves with His divine will. As we embrace His guidance and revelation, the plans He reveals to us are guaranteed to unfold as promised, leading us closer to our true destiny. Years ago at a conference, Pastor Bill Winston made a statement that has stuck with me: "Information is not enough to defeat the devil. To defeat the devil, one needs revelation."

This distinction is crucial. Information equips us with knowledge, but revelation—God's truth revealed in detail—empowers us to triumph over our spiritual adversaries. The world is rife with information, but true revelation is the breath of God that fills our spiritual lungs and gives life to our walk of faith. It's what allows us to stand firm when the storms of life rage, knowing that our foundation is unshakeable.

So, seek God's revelations and watch as He reveals the details of His perfect plan for your life. My prayer is that the word of God will become a revelation to you, unlocking the potential within you to conquer every spiritual challenge. I pray His truth will transform you and open the eyes of your heart to the hope and riches He has in store for you.

The Crystal Sea

Before the throne, there was a sea of glass, like crystal.
Revelation 4:6

A sea is one of God's greatest creations. It is always the gateway to something beyond. A child, for example, sits in the sea of its mother's womb before it tastes air for the first time. The Israelites stood on the floor of the Red Sea before they stepped into the "great and howling wilderness" that would lead them to their promised land. Joshua passed between two seas—the Sea of Galilee and the Dead Sea—when he crossed the Jordan River to enter Canaan. All of these seas sat at the dawn of great beginnings, but an even greater sea lies ahead of each of us, and that is the Crystal Sea mentioned in Revelation 4:6. You and I will stand on it before we enter into Heaven.

The Crystal Sea is the last of the great seas. In fact, it is the last sea that will ever exist. Is this true? The Bible says yes: "Now I saw a new heaven and a new earth, for the first heaven and the first earth had passed away. Also, there was no more sea." (Revelation 21:1)

For years I grew sad every time I read that. I couldn't believe heaven wouldn't have any beaches. Finally, I had a conversation with God about this and He revealed the truth to me. By definition, a sea is a body of salt water that is smaller than an ocean and is partly, if not fully, surrounded by land. It separates one land region from another. For that reason, the new earth will not contain a sea. God wants His children to live hereafter as a family without divisions. There will be nations and cultural centers on the new earth, but they will remain united under the banner of Jesus Christ and the geography of the planet will reflect that. There will be an ocean, but the raging tempests and angry slashes of turbulent, grey seas will no longer exist to separate God's people.

Here's an interesting thought: The Crystal Sea is also the place that you and I will imitate Jesus and walk on water as we prepare to enter into eternity. Is it a solid or a liquid? I don't know but what symbolism! When God rolls it up behind us and it closes in on itself, every memory of loss and suffering will be wiped away forever. As I write this, I'm reminded of all the science fiction novels I read as a youth. I was quite taken with the imagery—the flashing space vessels, bright lasers, and exploding stars. If that's what a human mind can dream up, imagine what God's New Jerusalem looks like. He is the Author of Authors and "no mind hath seen or heard what He has in store for us." (1 Corinthians 2:9)

Talk to God for yourself today. Ask Him, and He will show you things to come. (Jeremiah 33:3) Tell Him, "I'm ready for the Crystal Sea but I want to walk on water while I'm here. Please lead me into whatever you have for me next." I assure you, the sea will part, and the door will open.

Vision, Provision, Division

Write the vision, and make it plain upon tables, that he may run that readeth it. For the vision is yet for an appointed time, but at the end, it shall speak, and not lie: though it tarry, wait for it; because it will surely come, it will not tarry.

Habakkuk 2:2-3

The very mention of *vision* conjures images of a future teeming with possibilities, a spark that ignites a fire in our imagination. And while natural vision is the ability to see, spiritual vision includes foresight, the mental image of what could be. Think about children. They are blank canvases waiting for the brushstrokes of experience and education to guide and shape their futures. A spiritual vision is equally as exciting, but much like children, it won't thrive on its own. It needs provision—the resources and support to bring that vision to life. Just as a child's potential must be nurtured with education and care, a vision must be backed by tangible resources.

This principle is echoed in the Bible. In the story of Nehemiah, when he was stirred by God to rebuild the walls of Jerusalem, he sought the king's provision (Nehemiah 2:8), and God's influence on the king's heart opened the door to it. "And because the gracious hand of my God was on me, the king granted my requests." Provision ensures that the vision doesn't remain a figment of the imagination. It provides the necessary tools, opportunities, and support to make dreams a reality.

But what happens when a vision loses its unity and purpose? Division creeps in. Division is the fracture of a once cohesive vision, the disintegration of unity that undermines potential. It's like a building plan with conflicting blueprints—nothing gets built, and chaos ensues. The Bible warns of the dangers of division. Jesus Himself said, "Every kingdom divided against itself will be ruined, and every city or household divided against itself will not stand." (Matthew 12:25) Division can stall progress, create confusion, and destroy what could have been a beautiful realization of potential. Unity is essential for any vision to flourish.

Finally, in Habakkuk 2:2, 3, God instructs the prophet to "Write the vision, and make it plain upon tablets, that he may run that reads it. For the vision is yet for an appointed time, but at the end, it shall speak, and not lie: though it tarry, wait for it; because it will surely come to pass." Here we see the importance of defining a vision it by writing it down. God wrote His Word down, giving it life, legs, and a heartbeat. We should do the same, and then rest assured that provision will appear in God's timing.

Vision is the seed of potential, *provision* is the nurturing force that helps it grow, and *division* is the threat that can destroy it. It's a dynamic trio that requires balance and vigilance. With God's guidance, our visions can be realized, our provisions secured, and our unity maintained. Dream big, seek provision, and guard against division. This balance is the path to fulfillment.

Pearls and Coins

The twelve gates were twelve pearls; each individual gate was made of one pearl.
Revelation 21:21

We are told in the book of Revelations about twelve immense doors constructed from pearls, a material not generally associated with a building project. There is a reason God chose pearls They are the only jewels in the world created by a living creature and once a pearl is complete, extra steps are not required to enhance its beauty. The oyster begins the work, sustains the work and then completes the work all on its own. The oyster is God's creation. The pearl is the oyster's creation. By this we know that God is more a God of processes than a God of miracles. Yes, He can do miracles, but they don't satisfy the artist in Him. He finds the creative process as exciting as the finished product. So, where there is a pearl, there will always be an oyster swimming in the background. Where there is a plank of Cedar, there is a tree growing in a forest. If He mentions a diamond, there was heat and pressure somewhere.

Now, we understand that when Jesus sent Peter to pull a coin from a fish's mouth, he wasn't sending him to meet a miracle, but rather the conclusion of a process. The coin was already there. At some point, the fish had lunged at a flash in the water and a coin lodged in its mouth. We don't know when that happened, or who had a hole in their pocket, but God was orchestrating the entire scenario down to the second. Think of the coordination involved. This was the miracle. When the precise moment arrived, the man and the fish were in the same place at the same time and Peter's groping fingers found the coin Jesus had predicted would be there.

This is how our faith grows. We gain assurance that the needs in our life are not dependent on miracles. It would be simple for God to provide for us that way, but it wouldn't be the best thing for our faith. Who would want that anyway? There is peace in knowing that the years of our lives don't swing on hinges of divine rescue, which is what a miracle is, but on the thoughtfully conceived processes of a Master Planner. God has seen ahead. There are already pearls in the doors, coins in the fishes' mouths, and donkeys tied to posts. If we need a room, a man will have one. This has been the way from the beginning. Even Adam and Eve weren't miracles. Adam was created from the substance of the Earth and Eve was then created, pearl-like, from one of Adam's ribs. She didn't materialize out of the air. God so loves his processes.

When God tells us that He knows what we need before we ask for it, what He is really saying is, "Not only do I know what your needs are, but long ago I crafted the means by which I'll provide for each one of them. You will be astounded at how creative I can be."

The Mystery of True Godliness

Beyond all question, the mystery from which true godliness springs is great: He appeared in the flesh, was vindicated by the Spirit, was seen by angels, was preached among the nations, was believed on in the world, was taken up in glory.
1 Timothy 3:16

The nation of Nigeria is comprised mostly of Muslims and Christians, but mysticism continues to creep in at the edges. My family was very strong in their faith, and I participated in all the religious rites as I grew up, but I didn't make my public confession for Jesus Christ and get baptized until I was thirteen. That was in 2002, only twelve years or so after it was rumored that Benin City would host a global conference for witches. The affair, and its ultimate demise, was still the talk of housewives and gossipers everywhere. I don't know the full and true story, but witchcraft in Nigeria exists. How can this be when God has given us all such a glorious light to follow? Yet the contamination continues to spread. It's been reported that evangelical pastors are mixing Christianity with various occult practices in order to benefit from the lucrative healing and exorcism markets, which in the past were the exclusive domain of witch doctors.

None of this is surprising, though. For generations, people have lost their way in the vast, shrouded mists of life, catching fleeting glimpses of something wondrous beyond the trees, yet never fully understanding it. Then, one day, the mist clears, and the path is illuminated, revealing a glorious landscape that had been hidden all along. This is the revelation of the mystery of godliness, the unveiling of God's redemptive plan through Jesus Christ.

Paul writes in 1 Timothy 3:16, "Beyond all question, the mystery from which true godliness springs is great: He appeared in the flesh, was vindicated by the Spirit, was seen by angels, was preached among the nations, was believed on in the world, was taken up in glory." Here, Paul is outlining the core events of Jesus' mission—His incarnation, life, death, resurrection, and ascension—each a vital piece of God's salvation plan.

This is God stepping into our world and taking on human flesh, the ultimate act of love and humility. Who would want a counterfeit? Who would want to fellowship with a demon? The chasm between humanity and God has been lifted through Jesus' death and resurrection from the dead, and the ultimate victory over sin and death has been achieved. His ascension into heaven marked the completion of His earthly mission and the beginning of His reign at the right hand of God. In this mystery of godliness, we see the fullness of God's plan. Jesus is not just a teacher or a prophet; He is the Savior of all, the Redeemer, and the King.

So, commit to living out the truth of this message in your daily life. Embody Christ's love, grace, and righteousness, striving to reflect His character in all you do. Be a beacon of hope and an agent of transformation, sharing the good news of God's kingdom with a world in desperate need. In Him, the fullness of God's redemptive plan is revealed, and through Him, we are drawn into the eternal embrace of God's love and grace. Let this revelation of Jesus Christ shape your life and guide all of your actions.

A Prophet's Presumption

*When a prophet speaks in the name of the Lord and the thing does not come to pass...
the prophet has spoken it presumptuously.*
Deuteronomy 18:22

When a man has experienced a great deal of success, it's easy for him to start thinking that anything he does will be blessed by God. In the same way, it's easy for a prophet with a history of accuracy to begin to believe that he cannot utter a single wrong word. Few, if any, of his predictions have failed, so he stops waiting for the word of the Lord and begins to speak whatever comes to his mind. The prophet Nathan fell into this trap.

King David asked Nathan whether or not he should build a temple in which God would dwell. Nathan told him, "Do all that is in your heart, for God is with you." He didn't ask God, he just assumed that David could do whatever he wanted. However, God is more involved in our plans than that. He visited Nathan that same evening to correct him. God gave him a long and encouraging message to relate to David, but the core of it contained a simple instruction: "Don't build the temple. I want your son to build it for me." (2 Samuel 7)

This is a common error. We begin to trust in our own momentum and suddenly find ourselves out beyond God's provision and grace. When we're young in our walk with God, we're allowed this. Similar to the Israelites during their wilderness wanderings, we are led more by signs than by words. Eventually, though, we move from the wilderness into the gleaming, hail-pelted mountains and meadows of his higher purposes, where those pesky giants await. There is more at stake now. A reckless decision can put us within the reach of a Philistine sword, and the Philistines show no mercy. This is why we are told from the outset, "If you are willing and obedient, you will possess the land." (Isaiah 1:19). We could interpret this scripture this way: "If you are willing to wait until you hear, and then follow my instructions to the letter, you will have success in the thing that I have called you to do." There is no other way. Guessing, hoping and impatience only lead to failure.

I watched a Christian businessman rise and fall once. Eventually, he regained his footing, but he never reached the same heights. I asked him, "Why don't you do what you did before and follow the Holy Spirit's step by step instructions in your business transactions?" He was older by this point and his vitality was waning. He paused and looked at me, shaking his head. "I don't know."

A lion on the road had devoured his energy for projects and undertakings. A prophet in 1 Kings 13 encountered the same lion when he disobeyed God. God had given the prophet a message to deliver and told him, "After you have delivered the message, don't return the same way you came." The prophet didn't listen and sadly, was killed by a lion on his way home.

The armies of the Lord have a Commander and He wants to lead us to victory, but His sometimes-unconventional instructions must be followed implicitly. It may be "Shout and the wall will fall," or "Wait until you hear the sound of marching in the mulberry trees."

Whatever it is, no other act will achieve the desired result. Are you waiting for your instructions? They will come. We are told, "You will hear a voice behind you saying, 'This is the way, walk in it,' when you veer to the right or to the left." (Isaiah 30:21) Joshua heard and obeyed, and we are told that "the Lord was with Joshua, and his fame spread throughout all the country." (Joshua 6:27) God wants to make you famous. God wants to take you to the top of His mountain range. The world is a stage, and you are His champion.

Common Sense and Discernment

My child don't lose sight of common sense and discernment. Hang on to them.
Proverbs 3:21

I've often heard it said that opportunities in life rarely wait for the slow. You blink, and then bam! They're gone. Meanwhile, I hold fast to the wisdom found in Ecclesiastes 9:11: "The race is not to the swift or the battle to the strong, nor does food come to the wise or wealth to the brilliant or favor to the learned; but time and chance happen to them all." We need to be discerning to seize the chances God brings our way. God's blessing is an empowerment to prosper, and His favor opens doors of opportunity.

Early in 2015, I heard a pastor speak about the favor of God. The message struck a chord deep within me. I realized that I had probably missed out on many opportunities that God had brought into my life at various points. Yet, reflecting on this, I understood that due to God's unwavering favor, these opportunities kept coming back around. This perpetual flow of opportunities, borne of divine favor, offers endless chances—until, of course, the river runs dry.

I heard a story recently about a man who kept putting off paying his traffic ticket. The Holy Spirit was faithful to remind him to take care of the situation, but he procrastinated. Finally, the man had a dream in which a group of cartoon policemen were chasing him around in circles. Still, he procrastinated! Just a few days later, God's grace ran out and the man was arrested for non-payment of his traffic ticket. What a hard lesson.

God doesn't work on our schedule. Psalm 90:4 reminds us, "A

thousand years in your sight are like a day that has just gone by, or like a watch in the night." His blessings and favor are as fresh today as they were yesterday. God's favor brings us opportunities, but it's up to us to recognize and act on them. We must be discerning. Being discerning means seeing beyond the immediate and grasping the potential within the opportunities that come our way. It involves prayer, seeking God's wisdom, and being attentive to His guidance. Our responsibility is to be vigilant and proactive in seizing these moments. Along the way, let us not lose sight of common sense and discernment, for they are essential in walking the path God has laid out for us. If we remain vigilant and attuned to His guidance, we can trust that He will continue to provide us with opportunities to thrive and prosper.

Solomon's Thought Mines
(Sustained Focus)

It is the glory of God to conceal a matter, and the glory of kings to search it out.
Proverbs 25:2

Thoughts are not powers. The idea of *manifesting* is a popular trend now, but you can't force a thing into existence by simply thinking it. Thoughts can be harnessed, however, and you would do good to view thinking as a tool akin to the shovels, pickaxes, and drill bits of a gold miner. As an example, King Solomon was an astute miner. He was tenacious when he *applied his mind* to understand things. (Ecclesiastes 1:13 This is called focus. Focus *is* a power. One definition of a genius is "The ability to persevere and stay focused on a goal in the face of extreme challenges." Focus will keep you in your gold mine until every last flake of gold has been extracted, no matter the conditions. You may be isolated. You may be under pressure and feeling intolerable heat, but if God has led you to the cave entrance, you can be sure that your fortune lies within. It may be a witty idea, a business model, or an invention, but perseverance is the key.

A mighty man of God once said, "When the devil saw he couldn't have your soul, he set out to break your focus." That's because the rewards of focus are bountiful. King Solomon is a good example of this. He wrote 3,000 proverbs and 1,005 songs, as well as two books of the Bible. (Ecclesiastes and the Song of Solomon). Have you been that prolific? I haven't. Thomas Edison was another true miner. He spent two monotonous years searching for a filament that would burn in a vacuum. After 2,774 failures, a strand of carbonized cotton began to glow, and a world lit by candles and lamps became a world lit by light bulbs. Sustained focus. It's a power not reserved for just a few.

If we've sought the Lord and are confident that we're not chasing a vain pursuit, it's time to exercise *divine continuance*, for the temptation to quit too soon is bound to assail us. Spiritual warfare comes to mind. The devil loves to see us exit our goldmine prematurely. We tap into a vein of inspiration and eagerly scrape away the surface gold, only to let the heat and pressure drive us back to the surface where the routines of ordinary life put less of a strain on us.

I fell prey to this countless times when I was younger. I would receive a verse for a song at 2 A.M. and then go to sleep, only to find that the inspiration for the second verse and chorus was gone the next morning, never to return. The songs that will never be heard! I learned though. I once wrote 120 songs in a two-year period so I could choose the 18 that were the best of the best. It was a special project, and I wanted the pure gold.

Am I the only one? Maybe it's just me, but there have been countless times when I felt disinterested, lethargic, and even questioned what I was doing but produced my best work by staying with it. That snake is always there. He tested Eve with self-doubt. He shouted threats at Nehemiah. King Solomon experienced his presence too. The Queen of Sheba came to "test his wisdom with hard questions." (1 Kings 10:1) Who was behind that I wonder? If you are in the gold mine, but weeks, months or even years have gone by and you haven't gotten all there is to get yet (and I know you're tired), stay with it until the filament lights up, that final bit of inspirational archeology that will change the world. Stay focused. You can rest when you're done. Don't leave anything left in the darkness, never to be enjoyed by the world.

Work On My Mind

The Spirit gives life; the flesh counts for nothing. The words I have spoken to you—they are full of the Spirit and life.
John 6:63

Years ago, in a quiet moment of meditation, I sought God's presence and asked a question that stirred my soul: "Jesus, what are you working on? Work on my mind, please." His immediate and profound response reshaped my understanding forever. He answered, "Read my word! When you engage with my word—through reading it, hearing it and speaking it—you are doing more than engaging in an intellectual exercise. I worked on my disciples' minds the same way on a daily basis. I spoke to them, performed miracles, and sent them out to heal and cast out demons. These were practical lessons that encouraged them to think from a heavenly perspective and to embrace kingdom thinking. My words in particular washed away their legalistic and carnal thought patterns."

Continuing, He explained, "I wanted my disciples to see other people and to see themselves through new eyes. As they did this, they began to grasp a deeper understanding of me as their Father. My goal was transformation—to mold them into reflections of myself. As my words saturated their hearts, they were gradually transformed into my likeness. I am the essence of life itself! When my word abides in you, and you let it govern your actions, you will experience true life!" (John 6:63)

I was astonished, but there was more. "Read my word," God emphasized. "Let it set you free, for it is truth. Let my word work on your mind." (Psalm 119:130) In that moment of revelation, I was reminded more profoundly than ever of the power of God's word to reshape our thoughts, renew our minds, and align us with His divine purpose. Embracing His teachings goes beyond acquiring knowledge. Truths are internalized that lead to profound spiritual growth and a renewed perspective on life. Immerse yourself in Scripture! Allow its wisdom to penetrate your essence and pave the way for a transformation that mirrors the very image of Christ Himself. This is the journey of faith, where God's word becomes a living, transformative force that will guide you toward abundant life and eternal truths!

Normal

Who does great things and marvelous things without number.
Job 5:9

Miracles are not as miraculous to God as they are to human beings. It's the speed at which they take place that confounds us. If the water had turned into wine in slow motion, the feat would not have been as impressive. Same with the multiplying fish and bread. If we had been able to watch the atoms multiply through a microscope over a week's time, we would have yawned and gone back to bed. The mystery is in the epic, surging, lightning speed at which God is able to accomplish things. How does He do it? Well, He is not in a hurry, and He isn't nervously juggling pots and pans like a manic chef in an understaffed miracle kitchen.

His secret has to do with His location. He is outside of our time loop. We assume He's racing around like Superman or The Flash, but everything God does flows out smoothly from between His hands with meter, rhythm, and pace. Then, when His handiwork bubbles to the surface of the molasses of time—where we live—it bursts into existence like super-heated air. Even the *big bang* at the dawn of creation was carefully executed. Every hurtling rock and plasmic flare was painted into place by a slow and deliberate hand. There is no true chaos.

Here are some more things that appear sublime but are normal to God: stars that sing, bushes that burn, and floating axe heads. How about flying cities (the New Jerusalem), sticks that turn into snakes and dead bodies that come back to life? The list is endless. We are surrounded by and exist because of the power that does these things, but we live such ordinary lives. Why? If we're honest, many of us believe His schedule is too full to accommodate us. "I'm just one in seven billion. He's busy somewhere else. He saves His miracles for His chosen ones." We are His chosen ones, though! We may feel burned out in every way, but God is in us and His power is always just below the surface, ready to spring like a rising, fiery geyser into our slow-motion lives. The prophet Jeremiah was familiar with this leaden feeling. The pressures of existence were weighing heavily upon him, and he didn't care about singing stars, angels, or prophetic visions anymore. In a moment of frustration, he cried out, "I purposed to not make mention of Him, nor speak His name anymore. But His word was in my heart like a burning fire shut up in my bones and I grew weary of holding it back. I could do it no more." (Jeremiah 20:9) He was ready to quit serving God completely, but God reenergized him.

In times like these, we need to remind ourselves that each of us are miracles, only slowed down. It's the truth. We—the body of Christ—are water turning into wine, just slowly. We can't see it, hear it, or feel it, but each day we are becoming more and more like Him. The great cloud of witnesses see it. They are watching everything in God's time, not slowed-down time, and their cheers must be deafening.

So, don't quit. Take one more step forward. The molasses of life may be thick around your feet, but in actuality you are a miracle moving toward a triumphant victory at the speed of light.

Spiritual Physics

The Word of God is living and powerful…
Hebrews 4:12

When God spoke and said, "Let there be light," sound waves went forth. Those original sound waves hold all of creation together and are still going forth today. When God wants His voice to return to Him, He directs it at a reflective surface, which exist in this present creation as people, objects, and creatures. Everything that exists, from the smallest particle to the largest heavenly body, falls into one of those two categories and will respond to God's voice when it is directed at them. "My word that goes out from My mouth will not return to Me empty but will accomplish that which I desire." (Isaiah 55:11)

Now we start to understand the power of the sound wave of a word, as opposed to the power of a random noise. Words are containers. The sound waves of a word contain the additive of intent, whereas the sound waves of a falling tree contain only the rapidly decaying properties of vibration. Intent mirrors desire, whether good or evil, and is linked to the faith of the speaker. Humans are generally full of doubt, so most of our words fall to the ground fruitless. The potential is there, however.

Our tongues are like ship's rudders plunged into a sea of atoms and molecules. If we have strong confidence in our words, the molecules will obey us. Bodies will heal, storms will calm, and mountains will move. If we don't but have the stamina to keep saying the same thing for a long enough period of time, the sea is still rearranged, and a result is produced. Repetition doesn't give us God's immediacy, but it comes close to giving us His power. If we keep the same sound waves aimed at the same subject for a long enough period of time, the obstacle will eventually erode. "Whoever says to this mountain, be removed and cast into the sea, and does not doubt in his heart, but believes that those things he says will come to pass, he shall have whatsoever he says." (Mark 11:23)

Here's an example of how the power of God's word worked for me against a tornado. Years ago my two oldest children were attending a youth service on the opposite side of town when the weather sirens started blaring. I turned on the TV and watched as a large tornado began to track on a collision course for the building they were in. Without hesitating, I commanded the tornado to turn in Jesus' name. Instantly, the tornado swerved and made a very distinct loop around our church's block before heading for open fields. Nobody in the town was hurt by that tornado that evening.

I like what one minister said, "The word of God has one interpretation, but many applications." The words of God are containers of active intent that can be applied to situations as needed. Creation will always bow to the power that created it, which was faith-filled words. You have the same power. Build up your faith vocabulary and begin to use your words today. They are miracle producers.

Creation, Stewardship, and Influence

After gaining wisdom and understanding, the responsibility of stewardship and leadership over creation follows. What roles do we have as caretakers and influencers?

The Love Parable

Many waters cannot quench love, nor can the floods drown it.
Song of Solomon 8:7

The following is a parable that God gave to me. It has to do with love, marriage, and families, His greatest passion:

During the first, misty days of the beginning of time, a ladybug felt a vibration and turned to see God bending over a figure lying prone on the grass. The ladybug watched as God breathed into the strange figure's mouth. Immediately, it sat up.

"Who am I?" the figure asked.

"You're my son, Adam," God answered.

"And what's that?" Adam said, pointing.

"That's a ladybug." The ladybug realized it had been noticed and blushed.

"Is it just you and me?" Adam asked as he stood to his feet.

God nodded. "Yes, but only for a little while. You'll grow lonely and desire company."

Adam paused. "What's that over there? And what are all of those markings?"

The centerpiece of God's garden had caught Adam's eye.

"That's the Tree of Life. I carved the names of all the families of heaven and earth into it. See that mark?"

Adam squinted. "Yes."

God looked sideways at Adam with knowing eyes. "It says 'Adam loves Eve.'"

"Who's 'Eve?'"

God winked at the ladybug. "Oh, I'll introduce you soon enough.

Make me a promise though."

Adam stopped. "Sure, anything."

God fixed His eyes on Adam. "Don't change the marks. I carved the families in this order for a reason. A man for every woman and a woman for every man."

Adam looked perplexed. "What's a woman?"

God put his arm around Adam's shoulder. "Let's keep walking. I have a lot to share with you. Oh, and don't eat from that tree over there."

Have you ever carved a mark into a tree? If so, your etching could last for a very long time. The oldest living thing on earth is a tree called "Methuselah," a bristlecone pine that has withstood the elements of California's Inyo Forest for 4,789 years, and although its needles come and go, the scars of its seasons are still visible on its skin. Think of it. Methuselah has been around since the flood of Noah. It stands as great metaphor for the eternal sanctity of God's love for His "family tree."

In Ephesians 3:14, 15 we are told to kneel before the Father "from whom every family in heaven and earth derives its name." Mark 10:9 urges us that, "What God has joined together let no man separate." We are not to tamper with God's tapestry. Relationships are His sovereign domain, as we see all through the Bible, and we move into dangerous territory when we try to graft ourselves where we don't belong. The seal never takes, leaving us without a root system. We will experience withering fruitlessness until we submit ourselves once again to God's vine dressing. God has assigned us together by our names and when His purposes experience disruption and trauma through selfish actions, He is forced to take extreme measures to correct things. There is always forgiveness, but the damage done changes the tree rings permanently. Here is how the parable ends:

"As the ladybug turned to fly off, she watched a snake with jeweled scales and elaborately patterned wings slither toward the Tree of Life. The setting sun was creating a beautiful mosaic of light through the breaks in the foliage, but for all the beauty, she sensed danger. She couldn't know it, but the snake hated families. It would spend centuries coiled around their roots trying to suffocate them. But the Tree of Life is eternal, and although the snake would make trouble, the Adams of the earth would forever love their Eves."

Stewards Of Creation

*Be fruitful and multiply and fill the earth and subdue it, and have dominion over the fish
of the sea and over the birds of the heavens and over every living thing
that moves on the earth*
Genesis 1:28

In the opening chapters of Genesis, humanity is given its grand
blueprint: "Be fruitful and multiply and fill the earth and subdue it and
have dominion over the fish of the sea and over the birds of the heavens
and over every living thing that moves on the earth." (Genesis 1:28,
ESV) This command is the very foundation of our existence, often
dubbed the cultural mandate. It encompasses procreation, stewardship,
and dominion—a trio of responsibilities that define our role in God's
grand purpose. Yet, somewhere along the way, this divine mandate was
twisted.

The notion to "subdue" the earth has, at times, been misinterpreted
as a license to dominate other humans. Such a view is a stark deviation
from the original intent. The mandate was never about wielding power
over our fellow man but was about responsibly managing the earth and
its myriad resources. It reflects the character of God. It's dominion that
is loving, just, and merciful, not harsh nor exploitative.

This idea of dominion also extends to our relationship with animals.
It encompasses the domestication and use of animals for human
benefit, but it must never cross the line into cruelty or unnecessary
confinement. Proverbs 12:10 tells us, "The righteous care for the needs
of their animals"; a clear reminder that dominion involves kindness and
care, not exploitation. Remember Balaam's donkey? It was as self-aware
as you and I, and when God lifted the limitation hindering its ability to
communicate, it was not at a loss for words. "What have I done to you

to make you beat me these three times? Am I not your own donkey, which you have always ridden to this day? Have I been in the habit of acting this way?" (Numbers 22:28-30)

Humanity's true mission is to be stewards of God's creation. As someone once put it, "God wants the earth to be filled with those who are filled with Him." I'm not a fan of the frenzies created by modern environmentalist because they go about things in the most godless ways, using manipulation, coercion, and sometimes threats, but there are echoes of truth in their concerns.

As believers, we must recognize this and take the lead in the path forward. This involves working together both with believers and non-believers to foster sustainable communities that reflect God's glory. The mission God has given us is one of stewardship and co-creation. It's about nurturing and responsibly managing the earth. While we have strayed from this mission as a race, there is still time to retrace our steps and realign ourselves with God's purpose for the planet. It begins with seeking spiritual renewal, then engaging with our communities to contribute to a more sustainable, God-honoring world.

Lampstands and Influence

Ask me, and I will give you the nations for your inheritance and the ends of the Earth
for your possession.
Psalm 2:8

God tells us in Psalm 2 that He will give us the earth if we ask him. He doesn't mean metaphorically, but literally, only in an influential sense. World-wide recognition. But isn't this an evil thing to desire? It can certainly seem like it to a Christian. To be recognized on a large level sounds Satanic, but in truth, fame in itself is no more wicked than money. An unhealthy and greedy pursuit of it is wrong, but a platform of recognition can provide a believer with opportunities to glorify God in areas of society that were previously unreachable. We are God's candles in the earth, after all, and "men do not light a candle only to put it under a basket, but on a lampstand, so that it might give light to the entire house." (Matthew 5:15) The lampstand in this scripture has a very singular purpose. It is the means by which a light is raised to an elevation. The higher the elevation, the further the light is thrown.

Let's be open to God using us in a broad way. I once heard a preacher declare, "There are a lot of Christians called to be a celebrity but they're embarrassed to tell their friends. It sounds conceited and they will be subject to mockery for even suggesting such a ludicrous thing."

How is our vision, though? Is it elevated or is it low? Matthew 6:22 tells us that our eye is a lamp. Do we have a clear picture of God expanding our business, ministry, or social status beyond the limits that we currently operate in? Caleb had vision. He wasn't timid either. In Joshua 14:11, 12, he told Joshua, "I am as strong now as I was when I was young. Give me that mountain over there too!" He was eighty-five years old but was confident that God still wanted to elevate him.

Many secular businesses practice God-given wisdom principles without realizing it and dominate the marketplace. Coca-Cola, Nike, and Ford come to mind. There is no reason that your name or company's name can't achieve that kind of status too. The way to start? God says, "Ask me." Immediately, He becomes the architect of your lampstand and, beginning with the base, He will begin to elevate you segment by segment until He brings you to your pinnacle. Once there, your blessings will come straight from God, of that you can be sure. "The land you are crossing the Jordan to take possession of is a land of mountains and valleys that drinks rain from heaven." (Deuteronomy 11:11-15)

So, fix the continent next door in your sites and then "write the vision and make it plain." (Habakkuk 2:2) And as your influence expands, be sure not to neglect your lampstand, which was fabricated from the gold of your good character. It is comprised of "virtue, knowledge, self-control, steadfastness, Godliness, brotherly affection and love." (2 Peter 1:5-8) Wisdom will promote you but your character is your support. Now, get ready. You are about to begin your advance toward those far-off lands of conquest.

Shepherds For The Body

Then I will give you shepherds after my own heart,
who will feed you with knowledge and understanding.
Jeremiah 3:15

There was a span of years when I was hungry for God but was not in church. Looking back, I was like John the Baptist in the desert— young, adventurous, and independent to a fault, trying desperately to hang on to purity of character while the world continued to knock me about. I was sloppy perfect, and missed the mark occasionally, but God met me where I was. Slowly but surely, I left that wilderness. The first things to go were the TV shows, books, and music that had once been a part of my life. My new diet consisted of the word of God only and a greater sense of intimacy with the Holy Spirit was the result. Then, when God saw that I was committed to the high road, He placed me alongside of a man who was starting a church and said, "Help him." It was my first Kingdom assignment.

The church was successful, leading to a twelve-year stretch of serving alongside high caliber men of God. At the end of that twelve years, tragedy struck, and the pastor that was presiding at the time died. Zechariah 13:7 says, "Strike the shepherd and the sheep will be scattered," and they did. There was confusion and separation for a long time afterward. The membership of the church dwindled until there wasn't a much of a church left and I stepped down from the worship team. Suddenly I found myself without purpose again.

The very next Sunday morning I sat on the edge of my bed perplexed. "Where do I go now?" I wondered. The answer was right in front of me. When I glanced down at my Bible, a single line of scripture drew my eye. "I will give you pastors according to my heart, who will feed you with knowledge and understanding." (Jeremiah 3:15) I heard God whisper, "I have a place for you." And He did. It was just around the corner.

The next Sunday my youngest daughter and I visited a new church we'd heard about. After the service, I felt neutral. I was unimpressed. Later that week, I was fighting to stay focused on a difficult work project when I heard God say, "Buy guitar strings tonight." It startled me. I did what I was told, though, and then stared at the unopened package of guitar strings for the next four days. "Why did you want me to buy these?" The following Sunday I got my answer. The worship leader of that new little church caught me by the arm as I was leaving the service and told me he was losing his guitar player. Could I fill in for him? I said yes, of course, and that willingness to help turned into another five years of glad service, growing faith, and fulfilling relationships.

There is always a plan for the next season of our lives. If we need a shepherd, God will provide one. When it's time to be released, God will let us know. Geography, people, and time are important to God, with time perhaps being the most critical. The stages of every life include these: a *desert time*, a *time of shepherding*, and then a *time of manifestation to the world*. "To everything there is a season." Ecclesiastes 3:1-8. Obey the smallest command. I've heard it said that, "big doors swing on little hinges," and I have found it to be true.

Earthly DNA and Heavenly DNA

(Deooxyribonucleic Acid)

The Earth will also disclose her blood and will no more cover her slain.
Isaiah 26:21

It's 2024 as I write this, and more technological advancements have been made in the last 100 years than in the previous 6000. This fulfills God's prophecy concerning the end times given in Daniel 12:4: "Many shall run to and fro and knowledge will increase." Clearly, "many running to and fro" refers to planes, trains, and automobiles, and "knowledge will increase" refers to the sciences and computer technology. Isaiah 26:21 is also finding prophetic fulfillment in this hour. "The earth will disclose her blood." In 1924, band aids were just coming onto the market and television was still being tested, but here we are 100 years later, and a crime can be solved by matching molecular DNA left at a crime scene to a suspect. The victim's blood cries out, and science hears it.

This is all God's doing. In the past, criminals continued in their wicked activities because justice was slow in coming. "Because the sentence against an evil work is not executed speedily, the heart of the wicked continues to propel them to do evil." (Ecclesiastes 8:11) But things are changing. Criminals can get away with very little anymore and anxiety lives in their hearts. The human experience has always been this way. From Cain to Nero to Hitler, the wicked have always followed their impulses, but judgment is finally beginning to overtake evil.

This reminds me of an even greater scientific enigma, the mystery and power of the blood of Jesus. It is the strongest bond in existence.

It secured God's family for Him and is still the registering indicator of who belongs to whom. God dealt with me about this when I was younger and was dealing with some shame from my past. At one point, I thought that I'd lost my salvation even. Then God spoke to me. "If one of your children moved far away from you and assumed a new identity, what would a paternity test show?" The answer was easy. "A paternity test would show that they still belonged to me."

Then God became very pointed. "Earthly things are the shadows of heavenly things. If the bonds of earthly DNA are strong, the blood of Jesus that purchased your salvation is even stronger. A graft was formed, and it cannot be undone." It's true. We are so precious to God that even our hairs are numbered. (Luke 12:7) Incidentally, a single human hair can hold 90,000 strands of DNA side by side. Science tells us that the hair follicle itself is an excellent source of DNA and can provide a fingerprint to a family tree. Isn't that astounding? What God is really saying when He tells us our hairs are numbered is "You are mine. We have the same DNA." It's a family message. We are loved and nothing can separate us from our Savior and Creator.

Prayer, Praise, and Spiritual Empowerment

To bring everything together, we conclude with spiritual empowerment found in prayer and praise, which centers us on the vital role of maintaining constant communion with God as our ultimate source of strength and power.

No Stone Was Thrown

Let any one of you who is without sin be the first to throw a stone at her
John 8:7

The crowd gathered, murmuring with anticipation, and the atmosphere was ripe for a stoning. The religious leaders, righteous in their indignation, had dragged a woman through the dust only to fling her at the feet of a man who had captivated the hearts of many. This man, Jesus, was about to turn their world on its head. But the woman's world was about to be eternally changed as well.

The story of the woman caught in adultery, found in John 8:1-11, encapsulates a transformative encounter. The religious leaders had caught her in the act, yet the man involved was conspicuously absent. Stones in hand, they demanded a verdict, then watched as Jesus knelt down and began to write in the dust with his finger. His calm demeanor contrasted sharply with their fury. When finally He spoke, His words sliced through the tension like a knife: "Let any one of you who is without sin be the first to throw a stone at her." The religious leaders, convicted by their own consciences, dropped their stones and drifted away one by one.

Jesus turned to the woman. "Where are your accusers?" he asked. "Has no one condemned you?"

She looked up, "No one, sir."

"Then neither do I condemn you. Go now and leave your life of sin."

Jesus's response to the woman caught in adultery teaches us several important lessons:

☐ *Jesus Stands with the Condemned*: In a world eager to cast stones, Jesus stands with the shamed and despised. He sees beyond our sins to our potential for redemption.

- ☐ *Grace Triumphs Over Judgment:* Jesus's approach was not to judge but to offer grace, showing that God's love is not earned by perfect behavior but is given freely to transform lives.
- ☐ *We Have Been Empowered to Change:* When Jesus said, "Go and sin no more," he wasn't merely forgiving the adulterous woman, he was empowering her to live a transformed life. His grace equips us to break free from sin and live righteously.
- ☐ *Jesus Is Our Focus:* The adulterous woman's salvation didn't come from her own efforts. Hebrews 12:2 reminds us to fix our eyes on Jesus, the pioneer and perfecter of our faith.

When we focus on ourselves, we will only see our filth and imperfections. But when we focus on Jesus, He will set things right in our lives. Just as the woman caught in adultery found mercy instead of condemnation, so too will we. Don't allow others to condemn you. Release yourself into God's hands. He offers a new beginning, free from the chains of past sins, and will empower you to live a life that reflects His love and grace. This is what Jesus says to you today: "Look at me and find yourself in me. I'm on your side, I haven't come to condemn you. If you focus on yourself, you'll only see your filth, guilt, and imperfections. If you keep your eyes on me, I'll not only make things right, I'll set you free."

Why Should We Pray?

Let us therefore come boldly unto the throne of grace, that we may obtain mercy, and find grace to help in time of need
Hebrews 4:16

The look on Abel's face wasn't one of sadness; it was the look of someone lost in thought.

"Are you okay?" I asked.

He responded in a way that caught me off guard. "How should I pray?" he asked. "I thought prayer was a routine, but my friends make it sound like there's more to it than that."

Indeed, prayer should be a daily practice for Christians, but it's far from being just a mere routine. Prayer is the pathway to a genuine, intimate relationship with God. "Prayer is the wing wherewith the soul flies to heaven," is a beautiful quote that emphasizes the significance of prayer in our spiritual journey. Prayer is not just about asking for help, though; it is about connecting, confessing, and being in communion with God. Our reference verse encapsulates the essence of prayer— approaching God's throne to obtain mercy, find grace, and receive help in times of need.

Mercy speaks to the idea that God does not give us what we deserve. We see this vividly in Numbers 21:6-8, where the children of Israel were saved from the fiery serpents in spite of their disobedience. When they cried out, God provided a means for their healing. *Grace* speaks to the idea that God freely gives us what we don't deserve. It's the unmerited favor that empowers and sustains us, a gift that transcends our human understanding. We need grace to navigate life and to stand firm against the wiles of the enemy. And finally, *gratitude* tells God that we trust Him. As Johann Eckhart once said, "If the only prayer you ever say in your entire life is 'Thank You,' that will be enough."

Prayer is the master key. Jesus began His earthly ministry with prayer when He fasted for 40 days and nights in the wilderness. (Matthew 4:1-11) He also ended His ministry with prayer when He committed His spirit into His Father's hands. (Luke 23:46) Prayer is not merely a routine but a vital lifeline that connects us to God. So, start praying with a deeper commitment, knowing that through it, you will draw closer to your Heavenly Father and find the equipping you need for the next season of your journey here on earth.

Tongues and Enemies

And they were all filled with the Holy Spirit and began to speak with other tongues as the spirit gave them utterance
Acts 2:4

I desired to speak in tongues for a long time before I ever did. Years went by. Finally, the Holy Spirit brought the gift to me during a season of regular morning prayer, and it developed from simple syllables to a complex language fairly quickly. My walk with God has always been a supernatural one, filled with prophetic direction and divine encounters, but the gift of tongues brought with it a dimension of revelation I had never experienced before. Suddenly, I found myself praying with insight about circumstances I would never have dreamed I could affect. World events, celebrities, the spiritual realm—the Holy Spirit and I were connected on a more intimate level now and there seemed to be no limits in what we could accomplish together. I've heard friends tell of peculiar variations on this gift. A woman once told me that she would leave her body and find herself ministering to somebody on the other side of the world. This hasn't been my experience, but who am I to doubt her? With God, nothing is impossible.

There is a covert side to the gift of praying in tongues, where we operate privately, but there is a public and powerful side to it also. We might experience this when God has something to say about a situation but our understanding concerning the subject is limited. For instance, there was a season in my life where I came into regular contact with a man who very much disliked me. He even threatened to harm me a few times. I was walking past him one morning while he was raking his yard, covered with sweat and glaring at me in his usual fashion, when the Holy Spirit spoke to me. "Ask him if he needs prayer." When I did, the man dropped his rake and leapt at me. A moment later he was clutching me with tears in his eyes and whimpering, "Yes, pray for me! Please pray for me!" I laid my hands on him and prayed for him for a good ten minutes, mostly in tongues, and when I left him his entire countenance had changed. God had broken through some strongholds. We never did become close, but I watched from a distance through the years as that man became the spiritual head of a beautiful family.

If you don't pray in tongues yet, ask God to give you the gift. We are told to that all we have to do is ask. (1 Corinthians 14:1) The gift of praying in tongues will better equip you to be of higher service to God, as well as expand the channels by which He is able to download revelation to you. Once you've asked, be open, and in His timing this second language will become a wonderful addition to your spiritual arsenal.

Sing Praises With Understanding

Sing praises with understanding
Psalm 47:7

As the first light of dawn breaks and the sun graces the horizon with its radiant hues, nature itself seems to join in a divine symphony. The gentle breeze, the shimmering dew, and the melodious birdsong—all orchestrated by the Creator—invite us into a moment of peace and connection with God. In this natural cathedral, we are called to respond with something far greater than mere words; we are called to true, authentic praise. But what exactly is authentic praise? Psalm 47:7 tells us to "Sing praises with understanding." This isn't just about belting out a tune; it's a call to praise God with both our heart and our mind, deeply aware of His goodness, mercy, and faithfulness.

When Colossians 3:16 urges us to "Let the word of Christ dwell in you richly, singing with grace in your hearts to the Lord," it's emphasizing that the richness of our praise is directly tied to our understanding of God's word. The more we know Him, the more our praise becomes an authentic outpouring of genuine love and gratitude. It's like a child presenting a drawing to their parent—not perfect but designed with care and deep consideration. When we grasp the magnitude of the depth of God's sacrifice, our praise flows naturally from a heart overwhelmed by His grace. It's not about hitting the right notes; it's about letting our hearts overflow with the joy of knowing Him.

Moreover, praise is not confined to our singing. 1 Peter 2:9 reminds us that we are "a chosen generation... that you may proclaim the praises of Him who called you out of darkness into His marvelous light." Our entire lives should be a reflection of His grace, filled with acts of kindness, compassion, and a commitment to sharing His truth. True praise is a lifestyle—one that honors God in all we do.

Just as a child's drawing is cherished despite its imperfections, God cherishes our praise when it comes from a heart filled with love for Him. This heartfelt praise doesn't depend on our circumstances; it springs from the joy of knowing and experiencing God's love. And as we lift our voices in praise, something profound happens within us. Our worries fade, our spirits lift, and we are transformed by His presence.

Let praise be a regular part of your life, not out of routine, but as a natural expression of your love and gratitude. Let your heart overflow with joy as you celebrate your Creator, allowing His presence to transform you. Authentic praise is more than just a song. It's a way of life.

Angels

Do not forget to entertain strangers, for by doing so some have unknowingly entertained angels.
Hebrews 13:2

It can't be underestimated how involved angels are in the lives of men. They are always close at hand and are sublimely fascinated by us. To us, they are creatures of glory, while to them, *we* are the creatures of glory, bright spirits created in God's image but temporarily housed in fragile shells. They know what we look like, but what do they look like? Yes, the Bible describes some of them, and humans catch glimpses of them from time to time as well. I've seen them twice, and although I've heard stories of angels that looked like panthers, armored warriors and even children with wings, the two I observed matched the stereotypes we are most familiar with. On the first occasion, an angel appeared to me in celestial form, and on the second, as a man. Here is what transpired in my first experience:

I was newly saved and was making my way down a steep dirt driveway in the mountains of Colorado when I happened to look up. It was about ten o'clock in the evening, brisk with winter's lingering bite, and the sky was blazing with stars. Immediately, a moving object about three hundred feet or so above me caught my attention. It was an angel—long-haired, winged male figure wearing a breastplate and a robe. As he traveled from west to east between the ridges of the canyon, he kept a single arm stretched out in front of him. Maybe the inspiration behind Superman came from a similar sighting.

Two things struck me as being peculiar. First, nothing about the angel was rustling in the wind. His wings—swept back and silvery grey in the darkness—did not flap and his hair and robe remained perfectly in place.

Secondly, there was no heavenly white glow around him. Except for his skin, which was a sort of metallic bronze, the shades and hues of his outfit were not otherworldly. A few moments later he disappeared behind the crest above my parent's house and I was left studying the silent sky in astonishment. Was there anything else up there? Nothing that I could see. Whatever the angel's mission was, much like Gabriel in Daniel 9, he was moving swiftly to get there. He didn't even glance down at me. Nothing was going to distract him from his assignment.

My second encounter with an angel took place many years later in Tulsa, Oklahoma. I was driving to pick up some work supplies when I passed an old man hitchhiking. I pulled over and when he jumped in my truck, he gave me a funny smile and thanked me in an accent I'd never heard before. He was hitchhiking to New York City, he told me, where he was hoping his embassy would send him overseas.

When we arrived at the freeway where he wanted to be dropped off, I gave him some money, which prompted him to pause and take my hand. "Thank you so much!" he exclaimed. "God bless you in Jesus' name!" When he hopped out, I turned to glance at the traffic and when I glanced back—the man was gone! He had completely disappeared. This occurred right before God began to advance me into my ministry. Within two years of this experience, my home, circle of friends, and occupation had changed completely.

All through the Bible, humans encounter angels—it's a regular occurrence. I would like to suggest that when we entertain strangers that turn out to be angels, the encounter is precipitating change. The presence of the angel is heralding something. God is making the statement "I am with you," and a shift is about to take place in your life, just as Mary, and Abraham, and Peter experienced.

Included In The Story

After these things I looked, and behold, a great multitude which no one could number, of all nations, tribes, peoples, and tongues, standing before the throne and before the Lamb, clothed with white robes, with palm branches in their hands.
Revelation 7:9

We are shown many pictures in the word of God—imagery that reveals all of His brushstrokes from the beginning of time to the very end of it. The first thing we are shown is a featureless sphere comprised of basic elements. We see this in Genesis 1:1. It floats in space alone, a ball of raw material waiting for God's voice to shape it. Next, light is created, and the planet is given some features. Then the plant kingdom is introduced and space itself, empty up to this point, is populated with its various heavenly bodies. Finally, the animal kingdom and human beings are created, in that order.

We are shown these things, and then as time moves along, dinosaurs and other primeval creatures are discussed, including a dragon that is quite colorfully described in Job 41:19, 20: "Flames stream from its mouth and sparks of fire shoot out. Smoke pours from its mouth like a boiling pot over burning reeds." We hear of angels, wicked spirits and scheming giants, and their interactions with humans at various points in history.

As time advances we are shown a flood, followed by the creation of the various nations of the world, and then the devil is revealed is to us in lavish detail: "You were the seal of perfection, full of wisdom and perfect in beauty. Every precious stone adorned you." (Ezekiel 28:12, 13) Nothing is hidden from us.

As we continue to along, stresses begin to unravel the tapestry of God's plan. Wars occur, cities rise and fall, and then after a series of epic cultural upheavals, a solution arrives on the scene in the form of Jesus. We are told that He was not handsome or desirable outwardly (Isaiah 53:2), and his disciples were likely just as average in appearance. Jesus dies and is resurrected and the next thing we know, we find Him seated on a throne next to God. The disciples are there also, but are not so scruffy anymore.

Now, the view turns celestial. We are shown two female figures. One is clothed with the sun and the other is standing next to a red dragon. A character called the Antichrist arrives accompanied by a false prophet whose intelligence is potentially artificial. More fighting follows, then judgments and rewards and the banishment of everything wicked into a lake of fire. Then the end comes.

The universe is gathered up by God's determined hands and tossed away like a crumpled ball of paper. A new and better universe is created, a perfect one, at the center of which stands a city 1500 miles tall, deep, and wide. The top of it would extend into outer space if it were located on today's earth.

It's quite a story, isn't it? Along the way we have seen talking donkeys, a man-eating whale, floating axe heads, and miracles galore. No detail has been spared. Everything that is important to God in this present creation has been mentioned and described in the Bible, you and I included. Yes, we are there too. In Revelation 7:9 we are told of a great gathering: "After this I beheld, and lo, a great multitude, which no man could number, of all nations and kindreds and people and tongues, stood before the throne and before the Lamb, clothed in white robes and with palms in their hands."

If you look closely, you will see yourself in that crowd, smiling and grateful and glancing around you at the wonder of it all. Yes, that's you. In that picture, you are poised at the entrance to your true history where you will never again experience frustration, sadness, or pain. There will only be joy forever and ever. So be it. Selah. Amen.

Acknowledgements

We are profoundly grateful for everyone who helped bring this book to life. Each person's support, guidance, and encouragement have left their mark on these pages.

First, our heartfelt thanks to our family and friends, whose love and unwavering support anchored us throughout this journey. To the pastors and mentors who inspired and guided us with wisdom and prayer, we are deeply appreciative.

Our heartfelt thanks to NormaJean Lutz, who found joy and privilege in working with us on this project. Just as some love to clean houses, she loves to "clean manuscripts," and her meticulous care has brought clarity and polish to every page. Thank you for your sharp eye and skill in refining our words.

A special thanks to Mardy Ross, our "Unexpected Editor," for your invaluable contribution and editorial insights throughout this project.

Above all, we thank God, the Creator and source of all gifts. To Him be the glory. May this work be a testimony of His goodness.

To you, our readers, we extend our gratitude. We hope this book brings you encouragement, fresh insights, and a renewed purpose, pointing you to God's boundless grace.

To everyone who believed in us and helped make this vision a reality, we thank you. May this book serve as a light, stirring hearts, and inspiring hope for generations to come.

Made in the USA
Columbia, SC
01 December 2024

47767337R00107